Creative Quilting

THE JOURNAL
QUILT PROJECT

KAREY PATTERSON BRESENHAN, EDITOR

Creative Quilting

THE JOURNAL QUILT PROJECT

KAREY PATTERSON BRESENHAN, EDITOR

© Quilting Arts, LLC, Karey Patterson Bresenhan, and Contributing Artists

Quilting Arts, LLC
P.O. Box 685
23 Gleasondale Rd.
Stow, MA 01775
www.quiltingartsllc.com

Credits

Publisher:	John P. Bolton, Esq.
Managing Editor:	Patricia Bolton
Technical Editors:	Barbara Delaney & Cate Coulacos Prato
Designer:	Larissa Davis
Photography:	Dion & Company
	Cypress Media Works

Front Cover

Top row (from left to right): Peggy Schroder, Claire Waguespack Fenton, Franki Kohler, Terri H. Winsauer, Nancy G. Cook, Gloria Hansen, Mimi Wohlberg, Patricia A. Montgomery.

Middle row: Maria Elkins, Claudia C. Comay, Cynthia Paugh St. Charles, Jamie Fingal, Sherrie Spangler, Jette Clover, Carol Anne Clasper, Jean Myers Boos, Peggy Daley Spence.

Bottom row: Lynne G. Harrill, Linda Salitrynski, Del Thomas, Lynne Croswell, Ann B. Graf, Carol Perkins, Linda S. Schmidt, Rachel Roggel.

Library of Congress Cataloging-in-Publication Data
Library of Congress Control Number: 2006904395

Bresenhan, Karey Patterson

Creative Quilting: The Journal Quilt Project

p.cm.

Includes biographical references and index.

ISBN #0-9766928-3-X (paper trade)

I. Quilting 2. Patchwork I. Title

Printed in China

THE JOURNAL QUILT PROJECT
Table of Contents

Dedication

This book is fondly dedicated to my cousin and esteemed colleague, *Nancy O'Bryant Puentes*, who has been an important part of my life since the day she was born, who was by my side when our grandmother first taught us to quilt, and who has been behind me, beside me, and, often, in front of me, throughout my three-decade life in the quilt world. Like our mothers, she has always been willing to pitch in and help me finish a project when problems arise or time constricts, and this book was no exception. My love and thanks to Nancy for everything she does, but most especially for her unflagging encouragement, the creative ideas she shares so freely, her willingness to go the extra mile with me, and her incredible vision.

Acknowledgments

I most gratefully acknowledge the assistance of Nancy O'Bryant Puentes, Judy Murrah, Vicki Mangum, Pam Kersh, and Teresa Duggan in the development of this book and thank them kindly for their help. Special thanks are also due to Ann Graf for rescuing one of the QuiltPages from copyright disaster, to Ruth Moya who photographed each of the Journal Quilt installations at the various shows, and to Judy Smith, creator of the QuiltArt online community, for her continuing encouragement and promotion of the Journal Quilt Projects. Thanks also go to John and Patricia (Pokey) Bolton, publisher and editor, respectively, of Quilting Arts Magazine. Pokey, especially, has loved the Journal Quilts from the beginning, and they both enthusiastically agreed to take the risk of publishing this long-awaited book documenting the project and the worldwide movement that grew out of it. But my most heartfelt thanks must go to the 918 Journal Quilters who have participated in our five Journal Quilt Projects and who have opened their hearts and their minds to share their talents by creating 5,922 very personal QuiltPages, many of which are shown in this book.

—*Karey Patterson Bresenhan*
President, Quilts, Inc.
Director, International Quilt Festival—Houston and Chicago
Director, International Quilt Market
Co-Director, Patchwork & Quilt Expo—Europe

Foreword

It's easy to get so busy that, as an artist, you don't have time to experiment with ideas or materials.

At the end of 1998, I was thinking about the coming new year, and how once again I'd struggle to find the time to create a small group of art quilts in 1999. After I visited a friend from art school, now a prolific artist, I spent a lot of time thinking about how I could give myself more time and permission to "play." I remembered seeing an artist who, a few years earlier, had decorated a paper sandwich bag every day for a year. I liked her concept but knew that I did not have the time to commit to doing something every day; however, I could commit to doing something once a week.

I decided that I would make one small quilt each week in 1999. The rules were that each quilt would be 8" x 10" and could be made any time during the week, from Sunday through Saturday. As I worked each week, I could not throw out the original piece and start over with a new one, and I decided that there would be no limits on what techniques I could use. The purpose of this project was to play and experiment, not necessarily to make beautiful small quilts.

I continued making a quilt a week for seven years. I noticed that as I made these small quilts, the color and/or content changed as the seasons changed, and as I grew as an artist. Sometimes, the quilts became autobiographic, therapeutic, or both. After I finished one quilt, I usually looked forward to starting the next one. I also had more of a sense of accomplishment as my pile of quilts grew. As I continued to make my weekly quilts over the years, my creativity increased. It felt like a little switch in my head was turned on, and ideas came bubbling out. Not only did my weekly quilts improve with time, my larger pieces did, too.

It was very exciting for me to watch as the Journal Quilt Project started and took off. There was a discussion on the QuiltArt email list about creating journals, and I wrote to the list to share how I was making a quilt a week. List members discussed their interest in creating their own journals, and agreed that once a week was too much of a time commitment for them. Ideas were thrown back and forth, and the plan of creating a small quilt each month was met with enthusiasm.

Personally, making a quilt a week has been the best thing I ever did for myself, artistically. I know that making the monthly Journal Quilts has been a wonderfully creative project for the hundreds of artists who have participated over the years.

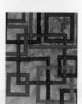

Each week I worked improvisationally with different materials, techniques, or ideas. One week I used unusually colorful dryer lint, another week I resolved the difficulties I had with a large quilt I was working on, and another week there was something happening in the world that I needed to express in my work. No matter what I created that week, it was all a part of a growing process as an artist and as a human being.

I hope that the Journal Quilt Project has helped all the quilt artists who have participated to experiment with materials, techniques, and ideas, and that we all continue to grow as artists.

—Jeanne Williamson
Fiber artist who, since 1999, has been making a quilt a week to document her life and observations, thus setting the stage for The Journal Quilt Project

Introduction

Journal Quilts are quilts that tell stories and quilts that break boundaries.

They are small, elegant windows into their makers' hearts and lives. At the same time, they are exciting doors flung open wide to a world of growth and experimentation. They personify the quilt artist's search for creativity and self-expression.

Beginnings

In 2002, when I created the first Journal Quilt Project—A Page from My Book—it was to inspire creativity, experimentation, and growth among quilt artists. The Journal Quilt Projects have been free-form exercises specifically planned to encourage quilters and quilt artists to stretch and grow by trying new methods—experimenting with color, image, composition, materials, and/or technique. Keeping an informal journal to record influences on their work and their own reactions to the experimental nature of this work has been an important part of each project, which was intended to show the participants' technical development and personal progress.

None of the Journal Quilt Projects have been contests or competitions; that was not their purpose. Instead, they have been open to quilters worldwide who participated in QuiltArt online (www.quiltart.com) and who signed up for the project, regardless of the level of their expertise. Each participant agreed to make a monthly QuiltPage no larger than the size of a piece of U.S. typing paper—8.5" x 11"—and these QuiltPages were then displayed in series on multiple walls that formed an enticing grid of color and design at the International Quilt Festivals in Houston and Chicago.

Personal Journeys

In the five years of the Journal Quilt Projects, 918 quilt artists have created almost 6,000 QuiltPages, of which more than 400 appear in this book. Their Journal Quilts have often told the stories of intensely personal experiences and reveal how the QuiltPages served as a catharsis to move quilt artists through desperately unhappy times in their lives. These QuiltPages telling of a time of tragedy or personal grief mesmerize the viewer as they read the artist's statement and then examine the piece that carries the story. Equally fascinating are the happy quilts, those that tell stories of joy—a disease in remission, achieving a long-delayed degree, the birth of a grandchild, a move back home, a wedding in the family. These personal glimpses into a quilt artist's life make the QuiltPages memorable. So many times at a show, we stand in front of a gorgeous quilt and study it, but we do not learn anything about its maker other than that he or she is obviously talented. With Journal Quilts, you often learn a great deal about the quilt artists by studying their quilts and the accompanying journals.

But it is the experimental nature of the Journal Quilts that is perhaps the most visually compelling to visitors. When the Journal Quilts are on exhibit, the display is not one that can be quickly seen; it requires time, study, evaluation, and close examination. Since the whole purpose of the Journal Quilt Project was to encourage growth through experimentation, the quilt artists have turned their imaginations loose on these little pieces. The restricted size worked well to free the artists from worrying about the time and expense of attempting new techniques on large pieces—they could try virtually anything in such a small format and find out if they enjoyed the process and liked the results without risking too much time, energy, or money.

From these experiments have come some marvelous and exciting results, in addition to the five spectacular exhibitions. Participating artists have received commissions based on their Journal Quilt designs; they have sold work, some for the first time ever; they have developed new classes and received invitations to teach; they have had invitations to exhibit in prestigious venues.

New Opportunities

Participation in the Journal Quilt Project has opened many doors for the artists, but the most important door may be the one to their own imaginations. Quilt artists, even those who are well-known, are not immune to losing self-confidence, hitting dry spells in their work, becoming bored with their art and needing a jolt in a new direction, or suffering a lack of faith in themselves and what they do. Beginning quilt artists are not always sure they even deserve the title of artist—entering

their Journal Quilts for exhibit at the International Quilt Festival may be the first time they have ever sent work off for display at any show, large or small. And the result can be exciting. For example, Jackie Mauer's words could have come from almost any Journal Quilter: "When I first saw my Journal Quilts at Festival, my heart soared, tears sprang to my eyes, and I felt that I had finally arrived in the art quilt world." The Journal Quilts have allowed every participant, experienced or beginner, the freedom to get past those mental and emotional obstacles and focus on producing an experimental piece that doesn't have to be right the first time, doesn't have to be an award winner, doesn't have to be the basis for a piece de resistance... it just has to reflect them and their growth at a particular point in time.

Artistic Growth

The techniques that can be seen in these 400-plus QuiltPages run the gamut from the tried-and-true of skilled piecing and appliqué to more avant-garde methods such as dyeing with shaving cream and attaching tin can lids by sewing through them! Photo-transfer, raw-edge appliqué, fusing, using Angelina®, metallic paints, embellishments of all kinds, discharging, over-dyeing, photo expansion, silk fusion, faux felting, found objects, layering sheer fabrics, beading, stamping—all these methods and products, among others, have been tried in the mixed-media Journal Quilts.

It has been rewarding to watch the growth of the Journal Quilt movement. Artists from 13 countries—Australia, Belgium, Canada, Germany, Iceland, Israel, the Netherlands, New Zealand, Norway, Poland, Sweden, the United Kingdom, and the United States—have participated in the five-year history of the project. Although several hundred quilt artists have participated each year, only 15 of them have taken on the challenge of the Journal Quilts *every* year, and their persistence testifies to the long-term benefits the experimental aspects of the project provide to the artists themselves. There are quilters all over the world now making Journal Quilts, based upon their introduction at the International Quilt Festivals in Houston and Chicago. Guilds in many cities, states, and countries have started journal quilt projects for their members, and individual quilters have joined together in small groups to pursue their own approaches to these very personal pieces of textile art. The QuiltPages have been assembled into books, sold, donated to charity auctions such as the one that benefited the victims of Hurricane Katrina, given away, framed, even used in university art classes.

Although we at Quilt Festival did not invent Journal Quilts—credit for that should surely go to Jeanne Williamson, who, since 1999, has been making a quilt a week to document her life and her observations—we are proud to have brought these quilts to the attention of the quilt and art worlds and to introduce them to many new fans. As these remarkable little quilts blanket the globe, there can be no question that the Journal Quilt Project has met its own ambitious goal: to encourage quilters everywhere to grow, develop, and gain self-confidence.

—*Karey Patterson Bresenhan*
Organizer and curator, Journal Quilt Project Director,
International Quilt Festival—Houston and Chicago

Series

The heart of the Journal Quilt Project may be

found in this chapter on Series Quilts, because it is here that you will see the QuiltPages presented in sequence, instead of individually. Although space constraints make it impossible to present every 'page' of each artist's Journal Quilt series, enough from each series has been shown to make it easy to follow the sequence. The quilts in this chapter were created by seven artists from the first project, in 2002; four from the 2003 project; six from 2004; and two from 2005. When the Journal Quilts were presented as an exhibition during the first few years, the quilts hung in a grid, so that the viewer could read across a line of quilts to see what a particular artist had been working on that year and the influences behind each QuiltPage. If the viewer chose instead to look up and down the grid, vertically, then it was easy to see the influences of each month on the artists, since January hung over January, July over July, etc. Later in the project the artists got to choose which of the quilts from their nine-month series would be exhibited, so monthly comparisons were not as easy to make.

Some of the quilt artists in this chapter have adopted a theme for their Journal Quilts: personal battles against cancer; a humorous look at the pitfalls of dieting; an exploration of portraits using different techniques; a reaction to a first-born son's Army service; a series of self-portraits; the heartbreak of a son's fatal descent into drugs. Others have selected specific items from nature—a sycamore leaf, feathers, women's faces—and have explored the vast number of ways to create art from that one item. Still others have focused on designing with the computer, creating textures with elaborate threadpainting, or delving into the artistic possibilities of inkjet transfers.

Regardless of whether the artist explored a theme or a technique, the series QuiltPages are remarkable in both their concept and their execution.

Christine L. Adams
ROCKVILLE, MARYLAND
Journal Quilt Project 2004

"My 2004 Journal Quilts explore 'Love's Many Facets' using vintage findings, images, and quotes. I used many of the same techniques in different ways."

March—"Friends"

"I celebrate girlfriends in March using dissimilar, beautiful, vintage buttons. March, the month when I lost my oldest son, is a time when my friends gather around me. Heavy typewriter letters were fastened by using waxed linen and beads with a knot."

February—"Lovers"

"During the month of lovers, I wonder how many men and women in other centuries espoused Camus' viewpoint? Here I have attached letters without holes using hand-stitched net pockets."

June—"Dreams"

"Before the crowds arrive, I take pleasure in the sounds of the surf at Cape May Point. Contemplating the waves is a gift I give myself. This time rarely fails to provide me with a sense of renewal. Rough-edged metal letters were sewed with heavy-duty waxed linen."

December—"Home"

"December is the time when many of us have thoughts of home. This vintage photo reminds me of WWI, WWII, and other wartimes when contact with loved ones is especially meaningful. I attached Scrabble® letters by drilling holes in them."

March 2004

February 2004

June 2004

December 2004

March 2004

Frances Holliday Alford
AUSTIN, TEXAS
Journal Quilt Project 2004

"Because I find copper so alluring, I decided to explore the use of copper in a grid format for this year's Journal Quilts. I challenged my left brain to make orderly, balanced pieces."

March
"Layers of organza, circles of copper screening, and accentuated quilting lines are featured in a distorted grid; the layers of materials give depth and dimension. I layered orange organza over the copper grid with angled quilting lines over the whole piece."

May
"After a trip to the Texas Coast, I used a painted rubber starfish covered in microbeads to accent my May piece. Timtex™ squares were stamped, edged in copper foil, and applied to a painted surface. Angelina® fibers were applied on top for luminescence."

January
"Copper tape forms a checkerboard in a formal, symmetrical grid over antique kimono silk combined with metallic glittered tulle."

May 2004

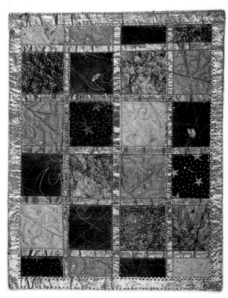

January 2004

June 2003

Maria Elkins

DAYTON, OHIO

Journal Quilt Project 2003

"Experimenting with portraits and how best to achieve them with needle and thread was the theme for this year's Journal Quilts."

June—"Judy"

"I painted the face with Shiva® Paintstiks®, then decided to quilt the face in a new way. 'Why not feathers?' I thought. I auditioned various possible feather designs by sketching on plastic placed over the quilt top. I then quilted it without marking the quilt top so I could maintain a spontaneous feeling. YLI 100-weight silk thread was used."

April—"Stephanie"

"I wanted to find a way to have detailed control over this portrait, so I explored ways to use colored pencils on fabric so they would be permanent. The watercolor pencils were covered with colorless extender to seal them so they would be washable and to serve as a wetting agent to smooth out the marks and blend colors. I used Derwent watercolor pencils; Setacolor colorless extender; and YLI Kaleidoscope thread."

August—"Christie"

"For this portrait, I tried to paint quickly, loosely, freely. I wanted this one to be fun! Only the most general outlines were sketched on the fabric before it was painted with Dye-na-Flow® and then quilted with Rainbows™ variegated polyester thread."

September—"Bethany"
(Opposite)

"This was the first face I painted. I liked it so much, it was the last one I quilted because I was so afraid of ruining it! This one is still my favorite...maybe it's because of her eyes. I used Tsukineko® All-Purpose Ink; YLI silk thread and invisible thread."

April 2003

August 2003

September 2003

Maria Elkins

DAYTON, OHIO • *Journal Quilt Project 2002*

"My plan was to try a different surface design technique, a different embellishment, and a different thread on each quilt. Each quilt has 100 percent silk fabric on the left and 100 percent cotton fabric on the right. Each quilt uses two different battings."

April: "I used the D'UVA® Erasable Watercolors™ full strength on dry fabric for the feathers. For the background, the watercolors were applied to wet fabric. On the feathers, glue was used to create the marks where the Jones Tones foil was applied. For the background, the foil adhered to the places where Bo-Nash powder had been sprinkled."

January: "I wanted to see if Prismacolor® pencils would be permanent on silk and cotton fabric after heat setting. This quilt shows both the washed (faded) result and the unwashed (brighter) result. When gently hand washed with

Synthropol detergent, the colored pencil faded significantly. The inner portion of the feather was colored a second time to show what it looked like unwashed."

February: "For the upper feather, the Tsukineko® ink was mixed with a thickener and applied with a brush. For the lower feather, the ink was applied with a foam applicator straight from the bottle onto dry fabric. For the background, diluted ink was applied to wet fabric."

June: "I made this QuiltPage specifically so I could use real feathers (from Amazon birds) as embellishments. I was also curious about comparing ordinary Crayola® crayons on fabric to the Pentel® Fabricfun™ dye sticks. The dye sticks, although available in only 15 colors, had a creamier consistency, were easier to apply, and were much brighter. The crayons did give a nice, soft result, and they washed well after heat setting."

March: "The background was splatter painted and the feathers were stenciled with a bristle brush, foam brush, sponge, rubber stamps, and rag. My goal was to create a variety of colors and marks using just red, blue, and gold paint. Createx™ Textile Colors, YLI Reflections thread, and Madeira® metallic and heavy metal threads were used."

March 2002 (Opposite) • April 2002 (Above)

January 2002

February 2002

June 2002

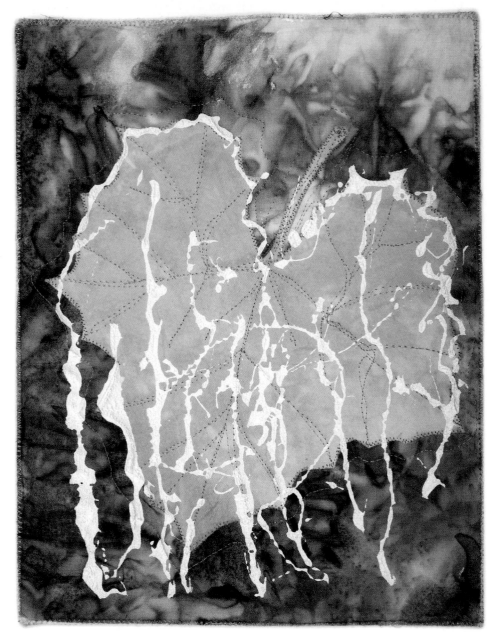

September 2004

Geraldine Congdon
PORTLAND, OREGON
Journal Quilt Project 2004

"I used a beautiful, leathery sycamore leaf image with a different technique each month. I scanned it, photocopied it, and printed with it until it was in shreds."

September—"Icy Sycamore"

"I discharged an image of the leaf onto a hand-dyed, lime-green fabric. The result was the icy blue-green leaf, which I fussy-cut and fused to the batik background. To enhance the icy feeling of this image, I mixed a pearl pigment with textile medium and dribbled the mixture over the leaf."

May—"Trees"

"I made photocopies of the sycamore leaf, a bare tree drawing, and Joyce Kilmer's poem 'Trees'. My goal with this QuiltPage was to collage the three different elements on fabric by transferring the photocopied elements. I transferred the images to silk dupioni using Citra-solv®."

June—"Swirling Sycamores"

"I wanted to experiment with color. I created a smaller image of the sycamore leaf and printed it in four different colors. I fused the leaves to their complements in a grid. I placed the leaves to give a sense of movement and machine-quilted swirls."

April—"Sycamore Transparency"

"I printed the image on white silk Habotai, fussy-cut the leaf so it had a gossamer look, and enhanced the transparent look by placing the leaf between layers of organza and tulle."

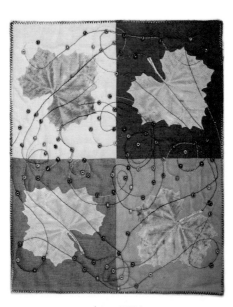

May 2004

June 2004

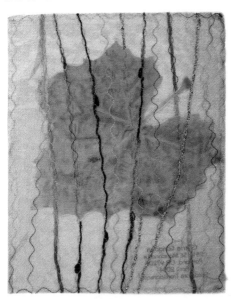

April 2004

January 2002

May 2002

August 2002

WHERE IS MY HAIR....
I CAN NOT FIND
MY HAIR......

HE SAID.....UNLESS
WE JUST GOT A
CAT, YOUR HAIR IS
ON THE SOFA....

July 2002

Stevii Graves LEESBURG, VIRGINIA • *Journal Quilt Project 2002*

"All of my journal quilts for this year are backed with a fabric depicting hands, because it took many hands to get me physically and emotionally through breast cancer."

July

"I am losing the wig everywhere. Plastic hair in July...yuck! I get a hot flash and throw the wig off my head...but only at home. I cut a 'wig' from a scrap of fur that came from a vintage fur coat."

January—"Good-bye to the Breast"

"Good-bye to the disease-filled breast. I will not allow myself to be consumed by the emotional and physical effects of this disease and the loss of a breast...but the effect is there. The surgical drain was removed a day before I headed off to Road to California to be judging floor chair and to lecture. Sheer willpower got me through it."

May

"The new chemo, Taxol, has caused neuropathy...numb feet and fingers. Dr. Stanton is worried about my quality of life as a quilter and wants to reduce the dosage. I tell him I want to live more than quilt...hit me with the full dosage!"

August

"Chemo is over, but radiation is necessary and more radical surgery next year. I'm in the car every day to get my skin fried, aka radiation. Five thousand miles have been put on the car going to all these medical appointments."

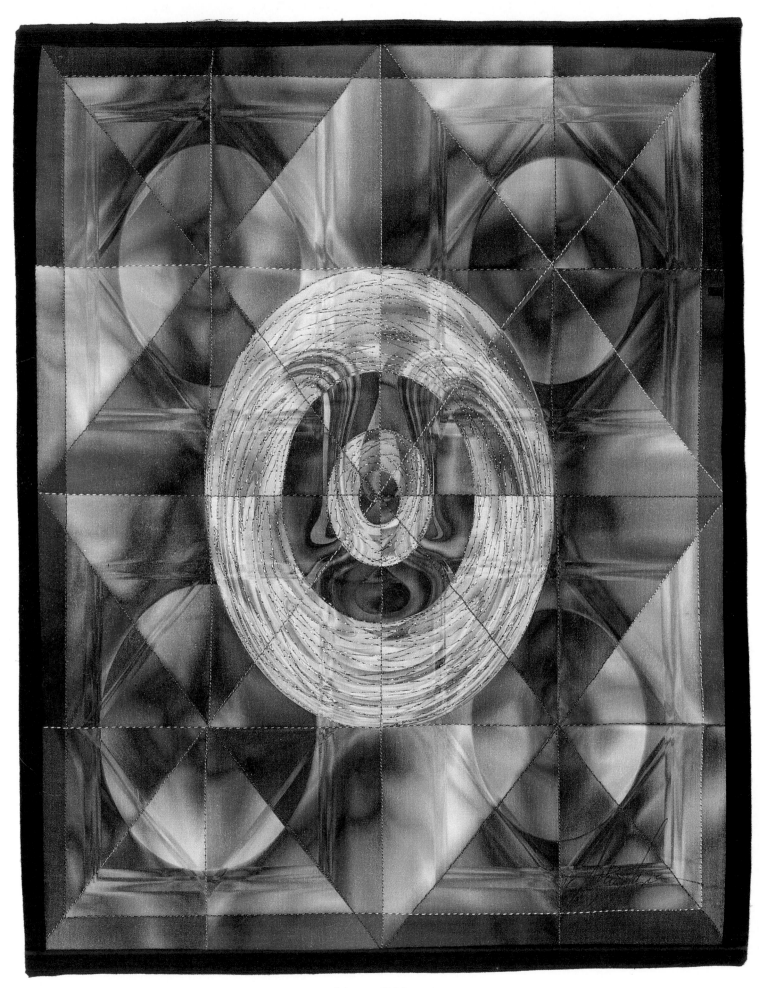

February 2004

Creative Quilting: THE JOURNAL QUILT PROJECT

Gloria Hansen

HIGHTSTOWN, NEW JERSEY

Journal Quilt Project 2004

"Images created with Photoshop® highlight the 2004 Journal Quilts."

February (Opposite)

"This design, based on a sketch, was created using Adobe® Photoshop®. I wanted to experiment with oil pastels over a digital print, and this is the result. First I created an 8½" x 11" document and divided it into four equal rectangular units. Using the sketch as a starting point, I redrew the oval and rectangular frame. I repeated this shape onto four layers, arranging each into segments of the 8½" x 11" shape. The image was printed on cotton fabric with pigmented inkjet inks, further colored with oil pastels, and machine-quilted."

September

"I find myself thinking about life and the push and pull of overlapping events. I designed this piece to reflect those feelings—overlapping circles, grids pushing, pulling, and distorting. Using the layers palette, I made a series of circles. Through a combination of coloring and blending modes, I emphasized the colors within the circles. The image was printed on silk."

March

"Excited by the QuiltPage I created in February, I tried another geometric idea, this time using oil pastels and Caran D'Ache® crayons to further color the design. First I created an 8½" x 11" document in Photoshop®, then divided the document in half vertically and horizontally. I then created three points from the center to the edges in each section. Using the custom brush I made in February, I colored this design using multiple layers to sweep in different color blends."

January

"I find myself thinking about when I used to create traditional quilts and took many months to quilt them. I started doodling a circular design with a traditional shape and wondered if I could re-create and color it in Photoshop®... I did. It is printed on cotton, painted with acrylics, and machine-quilted."

September 2004

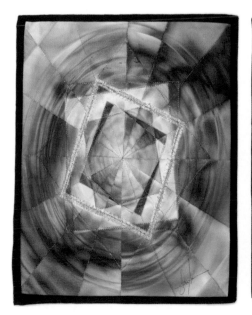

March 2004

January 2004

June 2002

Lynne G. Harrill

GREENVILLE, SOUTH CAROLINA

Journal Quilt Project 2002

"Self-portraits were my theme for the 2002 Journal Quilts. In creating these portraits of myself, I learned Paint Shop Pro® 7, Electric Quilt® 4, Micrografx Draw 5, and the use of the Bezier drawing tool."

June

"I decided it would be fun to use some of the image effects in Paint Shop Pro® 7 on a digital picture. The result turned out to be reminiscent of Andy Warhol's self-portrait."

September

"As a symbol of both finality and death, I have used a computer-manipulated photo of a skull, overlaid with chiffon, in remembrance of all who died on September 11th. However, as a self-portrait, the skull represents the inner self, the unique qualities of your personality that give structure to your life."

January

"This year in January, it was so busy that I felt like pulling my hair out. Instead, I had my hair cut in a new, very short, spiky style. I settled on a black background and no visible face to suggest how I had disappeared under all the deadlines."

August

"This month provided an opportunity to practice using the Bezier drawing tool in Electric Quilt® 5. I used a portion of Picasso's 'Girl Before a Mirror' as a guide for drawing the appliqué pieces, however, I gave the 'girl' spiky gray hair like my own."

September 2002

January 2002

August 2002

Jamie Fingal

ORANGE, CALIFORNIA

Journal Quilt Project 2003

"Commissioned work, challenge pieces, and my dedication to the Girl Scouts all play a role in this year's Journal Quilt."

September 2003 (Above)
August 2003 (Left)

August—"The Klimt Woman"

"This month's QuiltPage is a small version of the larger challenge quilt that I began in February and finished on our family's beach vacation. I read, embellished quilts, swam, and just enjoyed being with our family. I designed patches and adult-themed badges (Overboard, Card Shark, and Martini-Making) for the Girl Scouts' yacht-based Urban Adventure. My daughter and I came up with a recipe for S'mores on a Stick. To capture all this excitement, I used sequins, shisha mirrors and metal embellishments, a stamped face with acrylic paint, metallic fabric, and small squares of gold lamé."

September—"50th Birthday"

"My oldest stepson, Dan, began a new chapter in his life—a two-year master's program in computer science at Stanford. Jim went back to Harvard to start his junior year, and Jen started back to middle school as an 8th grader. I turned 50! Wow! I used my September QuiltPage for my actual birthday invitation, and the man of my dreams and the love of my life sent me and my friend to Quilt Festival in Houston for my birthday gift!"

May 2003

May—Make New Friends

"I was commissioned to make a quilt similar to "The Klimt Woman", but larger and with two women. Too fun! I chaired the Girl Scouts' Silver and Gold Awards Ceremony in Orangewhere more than 51 girls earned leadership recognition—a record year. I also designed a logo for the Girl Scouts of Orange County's first fundraiser, their Urban Adventure. It was my version of Juliette Low in adventure gear. It was so exciting to see my artwork in print and on their website. Batik fabrics, ribbon, gold metallic fabric, gold and silver lamé, rubber stamping, and photo transfer for the text were used here."

February—On the Inside, Looking Out

"This month I began work on a challenge quilt for Quilts on the Wall: Fiber Artists, in which the quilt would be vertically oriented with a contrast line about midway from the top. My plan was to design a Gustav Klimt-inspired woman, where the contrast line would be at her shoulders. My Cadette Troop attended Girl Scout camp in the mountains, and I took my Klimt Woman quilt to work on. The adults asked 'where are the blocks?' and the girls were absolutely enthralled that a quilt could be considered 'art.' I used batik, hand-dyed fabrics, rubber stamping, fusing, and machine quilting."

February 2003

August 2002

Margaret Hunt

CLARKS HILL, SOUTH CAROLINA

Journal Quilt Project 2002

"In 2002 I took a lot of digital pictures everywhere I went to document my year with my trusty old Sony Mavica®...it was almost new then. All of these QuiltPages started out with one of my own digital pictures that was printed on pima cotton and treated with Bubble Jet Set®. Each QuiltPage was heavily threadpainted using free-motion machine work, with a wide variety of threads to enhance the picture. The colors are mostly muted, with some vivid exceptions, including: blue, brown, green, teal, pink, and gray. None of the 2002 Journal Quilt pieces are quilted."

August—"French Section Opryland" *(Opposite)*

"The photo was printed onto cotton; the lapped border is dark batik with ¼" wide batik fabric binding that is mitered at the corners. I used Bubble Jet Set® photo printing."

July—"Edisto Beach Rocker"

"Colors used here include gray, white, iridescent black, yellow variegated to green, pink, and green. Solids and batiks are used in the borders."

January—"Winter Trees"

"The blues, grays, silvers, and purples of winter predominate for this month."

September—"Summer's End"

"Magnificent sunsets dictate the colors of this QuiltPage."

July 2002

January 2002

September 2002

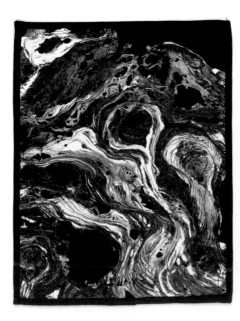

June 2003

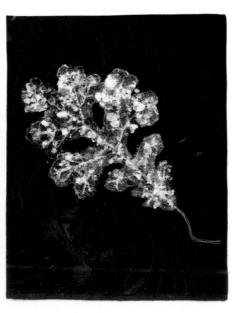

May 2003

January 2003

Leslie Tucker Jenison
SAN ANTONIO, TEXAS

Journal Quilt Project 2003

"This year's Journal Quilt was the product of many different, dissimilar experiments. I was particularly interested in developing uses for non-traditional materials in quilts."

June—"Amelia"

"This image was reproduced onto fabric from an original oil painting of mine based on a public-domain photo from Amelia Earhart's first pilot's license. (Amelia and I are both from Kansas, and we're both pilots!) With this QuiltPage, I wanted to see if I could manipulate the image by using free-motion embroidery."

May—"Malachite"

"After seeing a gorgeous malachite pendant, I decided to explore combining non-traditional materials to achieve the look of malachite. Post-consumer Tyvek® (from a used mailing envelope) was painted with a thick layer of artist's acrylic paint, and the paint was sculpted with a faux finish paint tool. The Tyvek® was sewn with cotton thread following the contours of the paint."

January—"Ice Storm"

"In South Texas, an ice storm is an event since it happens so rarely. This quilt attempts to capture the experience of viewing ice on foliage. I used my hand-dyed cotton, then bleach-discharged and over-painted it with fabric paint using a Thermofax® screen. To achieve the look of ice frozen onto the leaf, I glued individual pieces of mica, a non-traditional material for use on textiles, onto the leaf surface, then quilted over it when dry."

September—"Fall Seed Pods"
(Opposite)

"This QuiltPage is an exercise using unconventional types of silk. I attempted to create the mood of fall with the colors and forms within the piece. Part of a silk handkerchief was machine-stitched onto the batting and backing, and hand-dyed trim was couched over it. I cut open the hand-dyed silk cocoons, removed the unfortunate occupants, and appliquéd the pods. The leaves were created by sandwiching unwoven silk between Solvy™ layers, satin stitching around the edges, and stitching veins in the leaves."

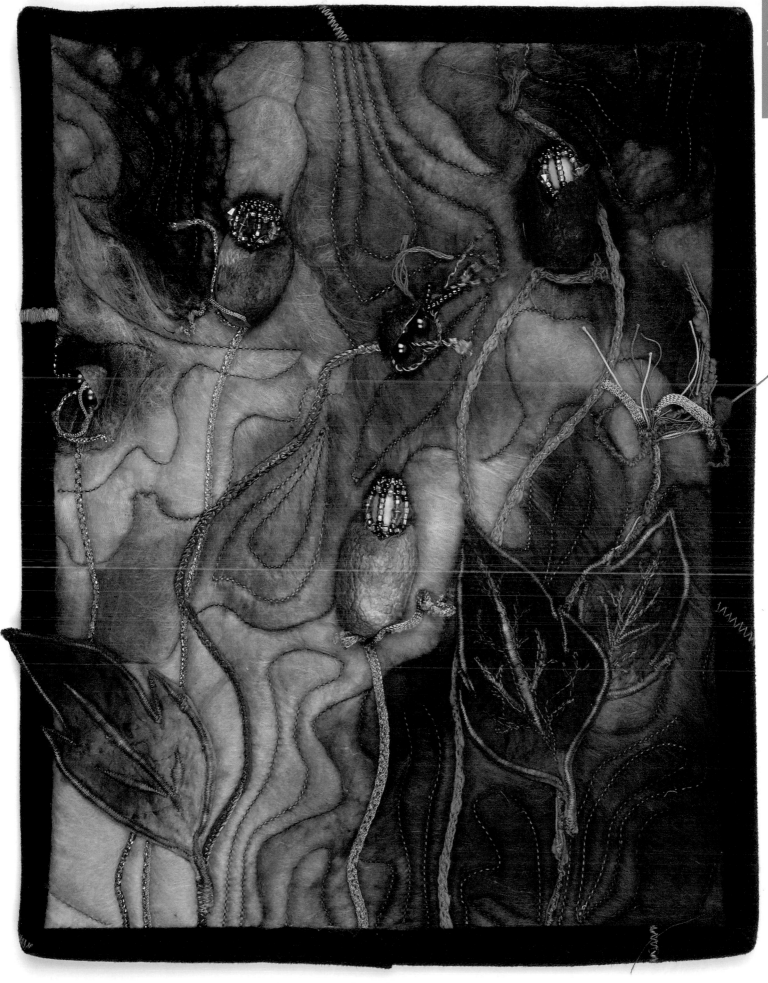

September 2003

August 2005

Diane Kopec

BABYLON, NEW YORK

Journal Quilt Project 2005

"Last year (2004) was an incredible year for me since I was diagnosed and treated for cancer. I had to live through the 'anniversaries' of the events of 2004 and used these special dates as inspiration for my 2005 Journal Quilt."

August—"Chemo Brain"
(Opposite)

"My last chemo session was August 25th. By this time I was really wiped out from the treatment and frustrated that being a 'multi-tasker' was not possible anymore. I finally discovered that just painting on the fusible with acrylics and 'sketching' with the needle was liberating for me. I didn't know how to portray the separation I felt from my old self, but this image does just that."

February—"February 25: You Have Cancer"

"I wrote a piece about my memory of that day—the day my cancer journey began. The colors in the fabric are intense with emotion, just like that day."

March—"March 31: First Chemo Session"

"They say my cancer is so small, less than one centimeter. This image is my version of a royalty free photo I found of cells being magnified millions of times. Fused and altered with colored pencils, it was therapeutic for me to create and reflect on my first chemo session when I had an allergic reaction to Taxol. I came back the next day—April Fool's Day (how appropriate!)—and finished the chemo with flying colors. And here are the colors! I beat my cancer on the first day."

April—"Bad Hair Days"

"My hair started falling out in clumps right after my second chemo treatment. I just had Chris buzz it all off after the second day of bad hair. This image was painted on fusible and transferred to pima cotton. I added Angelina® fibers, which looked like the clumps of hair, and tulle and fused them to the painted image, then quilted. The metallic effect of the fused Angelina® fibers was a pleasant surprise—seeing me bald was not so pleasant."

February 2005

March 2005

April 2005

July 2004

Kathleen McCabe

CORONADO, CALIFORNIA

Journal Quilt Project 2004

"My Journal Quilt for 2004 told the tragic story of my son and his drug addiction."

January—"Poppies"

"I had to tell my son he was not invited home for Christmas because of his active heroine addiction. 'I cannot bear to see you this way,' I told him."

March—"Dwelling Place"

"For the most part, my son lived 'outdoors' and ate at churches and other charity places. His clothing and possessions were what he had on his back."

April—"Is There Light at the End of the Tunnel?"

"The day after his 25th birthday, my son checked into a detox unit. 'Not on my birthday, but for my birthday,' he told me. He was scheduled to go into drug treatment in nine days."

July—"Laying Fears to Rest"

"When my son was taken to the drug treatment facility he walked in the front door and out the back door. He was arrested and served 40 days in jail. He died of an accidental overdose the day he was released from jail, July 22. I had done this piece before he died, trying to dispel the fears that haunted me daily."

January 2004

March 2004

April 2004

Kim Ritter

HOUSTON, TEXAS

Journal Quilt Project 2002

"This year's Journal Quilt reflects a continuation and further development of techniques and processes that I have been incorporating into my work."

March—"Thaw"

"Still reeling, my family is in shock. My father's remains are identified by the custom-made cowboy boots he was wearing when taken to the crematorium. They have his name stitched inside. The ice begins to thaw."

April—"Steaming"

"Now it's time to get mad. Steaming is more like it. How could anyone do this to our family? To hundreds of families? 'Steaming' is computer-printed silk, applied to a ground of painted and printed silk."

May—"Wave"

"The wave of summer is coming to wash away the remnants of a bad winter. 'Wave' is acrylics on canvas with machine quilting. Metallic paints on Tyvek® heated with a heat gun to bubble slightly were also used for this QuiltPage."

June—"Head in the Clouds"

"Summer is a time to have your head in the clouds and look forward to the sunny months ahead. To catch that feeling of floating in the clouds, a scan of one of my face line drawings allowed me to fill the spaces with bit-map patterns. 'Head in the Clouds' is digital imagery on inkjet-printed silk. The background is a digitally manipulated picture of a nautilus shell. The face was appliquéd onto the background by machine and machine-quilted."

April 2002

May 2002

March 2002

June 2002

April 2002

Karen Stiehl Osborn

OMAHA, NEBRASKA

Journal Quilt Project 2002

"This was a year of experimentation and new experiences reflected in my Journal Quilts for 2002."

April—"Whispers in the Woods" (Opposite)

"This month was an experiment in unplanned strip-piecing with scraps. The autumn colors lent themselves to a feeling of leaves falling quietly in the woods, which was accented with appliquéd leaves and beads. When I finished this journal, it was a half-inch short. Ever resourceful, I fussy-cut some wavy fabric and stitched it to the bottom of the journal to make it longer...ironically, that's what most people love!"

February—"Celebration of Marriage"

"February is the month for valentines and the month of my anniversary—a perfect month for hearts. The colors are bright and happy—reflecting the blessing it has been to share my life with my husband. He truly is my best friend."

March—"Moonlight Mambo"

"In March 1994 I spent eight days in Jamaica. It was my first trip to the Caribbean, and I fell in love with the bright colors of clothing and the reggae music. The colorful fabric in the center of this QuiltPage was purchased in a fabric market in downtown Montego Bay. Every year my thoughts return to the islands, and my heart longs for the sound of the steel drums."

January—"The Loss"

"January is the beginning of a new year—my first year without Dad. He was my hero, and the loss I feel is immeasurable. The larger circle is representative of him drifting upward, towards heaven; while the four smaller circles symbolize the four children he left behind. We are drifting aimlessly...alone."

February 2002

March 2002

January 2002

Surfacing

January 2002

Creative Quilting: THE JOURNAL QUILT PROJECT

Lesley Riley

BETHESDA, MARYLAND

Journal Quilt Project 2002

"This is going to be a year of adventure for me as I venture out into the world to share myself and my art. Twelve women, 12 months, endless possibilities. Another project is just beginning and we all feel that it will have a major impact on our lives, and if successful, the lives of many women. I have wanted to collaborate with other artists for many, many years, and it is finally happening. A circle of women, artists, peers—the realization of a dream."

January (Opposite)

"I am finally surfacing again—out from under deadlines, commitments, responsibilities, term papers, and holidays. I know that the more you have to do, the more you get done, but I am enjoying this month with relatively nothing to do. For this QuiltPage, I used my new inkjet transfer technique with direct printing on fabric. The progression of layers as well as the overlapping of sheer fabric and image creates the feeling of a woman surfacing from the water."

February

"Back out in the world. I chose the quote and image on this QuiltPage because this is the year I will share my vision. The need to reach out to others is greater than my fears of failure or rejection. I wanted to contrast the familiar with the unknown and chose these fabrics to convey that notion: the old-fashioned checkered napkin and cabbage rose print against the cutting edge black-and-white print. It's yesterday riding on tomorrow...just like me."

March

"I am bold. I am trying new things. This meticulously painted and rusted fabric has been waiting for me to find a place for it; the inspiration finally caught up with the vision. The experiment: to see if my inkjet transfer process would work on this surface. *Success!*"

April

"Many of the paths I am on have come together this month, and the journey is becoming more purposeful, more direct. I feel more confident with every step that the effort is indeed taking me where I want to go. The joy of it is that there are so many new adventures along the way when you move in the direction of your dreams."

When I dare to be powerful - to use my strength in the service of my vision, then it becomes less & less important whether I am afraid.
Audre Lorde

February 2002

March 2002

April 2002

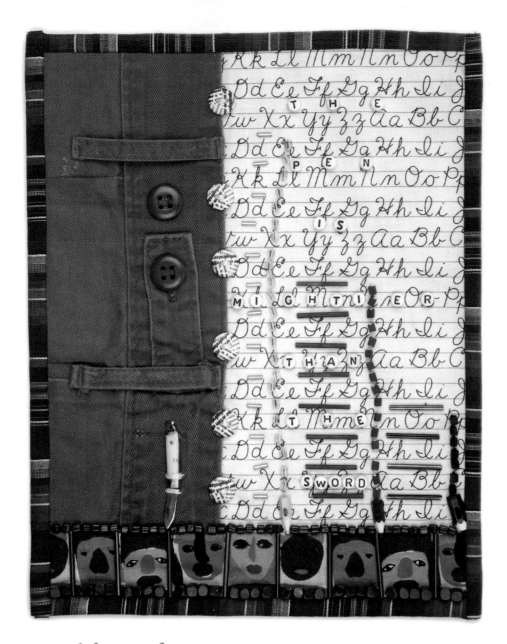

January 2004 (Above)
February 2004 (Left)

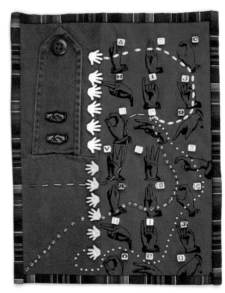

May 2004

Rachel Roggel

REHOVOT, ISRAEL

Journal Quilt Project 2004

"My 2004 Journal Quilt is entitled 'Fatigued'. I live in Israel. War is grueling and takes its toll piece by piece. These QuiltPages all incorporate pieces of retired Israeli Army uniforms."

February—"The Pen is Mightier than the Sword"

"The waistband is where you fasten your weapon. Imagine, instead, that you were hooking a pen there. How would our world be different?"

January—"The Lost Submarine"

"Semaphores are one way to communicate at sea, but the submarine Dakar's distress call never got through. Instead, the sub lay hidden deep in a pocket of the sea for 31 years, until even the bones of its crew were lost. Dakar vanished January 25, 1968, on its way from Portsmouth, England, to Haifa, Israel, and was found in 1999 near Crete and under 2,900 meters of water."

May—"You Can't Shake Hands with a Clenched Fist"

"Consider two armies...so many hands, pointing in opposite directions, never coming together. How would it be if the captain's bars on your epaulet came from building alliances instead of tearing them down?"

March—"P.O.W./M.I.A."

"When you raise your arms in surrender, the vent in the underarm is revealed. After that, it's simply a matter of luck whether you're released in five days, or 10, or 50—or not at all. A t-shirt with the names of all Israeli MIAs on a dog-tag design was used."

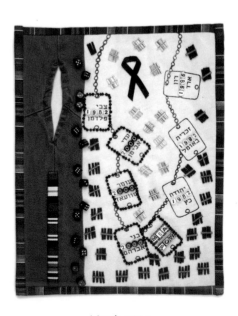

March 2004

Journal Quilt Project 2002

"What's a mother to do when her first-born starts his mandatory army service? That is the theme of my 2002 Journal Quilt. My answer was to use as many worry dolls as I could find to ease my mind and his, and to use parts of my husband's Israeli Army uniform, since he is about to end his reserve duty. Even the rifle cleaning flannel was used as binding."

January—"Women prevent the threads of life from being broken"

"We all need to practice mending—mending hearts, mending fences, mending relationships—and so my personal mending kit from my time in the Israeli Air Force is part of this QuiltPage."

February—"Pray for peace!"

"The weeks of terror attacks made me think of William Blake's poem 'The Divine Image' as found in SONGS OF INNOCENCE.

To Mercy, Pity, Peace, and Love
All pray in their distress...
For Mercy has a human heart,
Pity, a human face:
And Love, the human form divine,
And Peace, the human dress."

June

"Don't lose your buttons, especially those that conceal the family jewels."

September

"The soldier above all other people prays for peace."

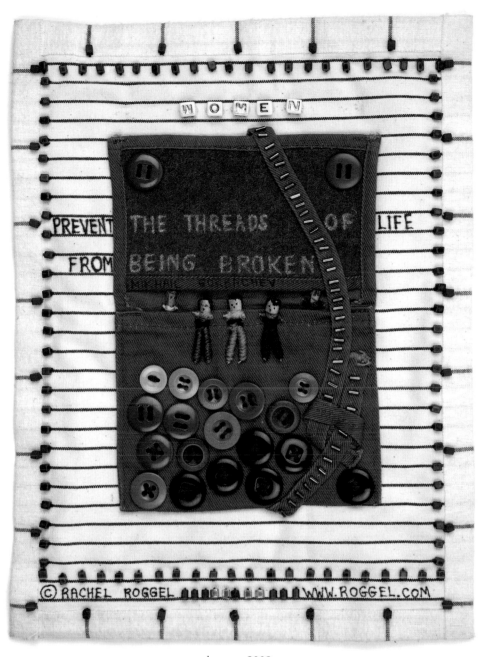

January 2002

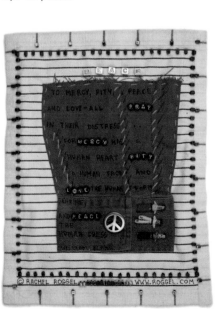

February 2002

June 2002

September 2002

September 2003

February 2003 (Above) • April 2003 (Above right)

August 2003

Mimi Wohlberg

MERRICK, NEW YORK • *Journal Quilt Project 2003*

"The problem I was having with my heel and hip in 2003 made my Journal Quilt focus easy—I focused on where my feet took me each month of the year."

September *(Opposite)*

"The deadline for the last QuiltPage was upon me. Late into the night I stitched, finally finishing one of the most fascinating, challenging series I have ever done. The background is a wholecloth with the window area and frame painted on beads used to represent machine parts, and my foot working away...finally feeling fine!"

February

"Spending time on the beach contemplating sunsets always makes one feel better. This QuiltPage uses fabric printing, scanning, fabric painting, beading, and even two-sided loose appliqué."

April

"In April I went to Chicago to the International Quilt Festival, an amazing quilt show. The background here is the result of a watercolor painting technique using fabric paints on wet fabric in a painterly manner."

August

"In August, a cousin's wedding on the beach at Westhampton, New York, turned into the most romantic, beautiful experience, as it was the night of The Blackout—August 14, 2003!"

March 2005

Sylvia M. Weir
BEAUMONT, TEXAS
Journal Quilt Project 2005

"Who among us has not fallen victim to the tyranny of a diet? And so, my 2005 Journal Quilt is 'Diary of a Diet'. Lutradur® was used as the background for each page. I prepped it with a mix of gel medium and acrylic paint. It was then cut into pages and fed through the printer. I chose terms that referred to weight loss and then used raw machine appliqué to add the figures. Decorative machine stitches, ribbons, and paper ephemera were also added as needed."

March

"Where have the first three months of this year gone? It's my birthday and I'm still fat!"

February

"First I assess my current condition. What a piglet!"

April

"I begin by eating mostly lettuce. And now I'm turning into a large head of lettuce. Maybe I should dye my hair red, then I wouldn't be green!"

May

"I'm dreaming of chocolate! Mostly because I can't have any on this blankety-blank diet!"

February 2005

April 2005

May 2005

Stories

Anyone who loves quilts knows that quilts tell stories. They're one of the best of the material culture objects used in universities to teach cultural influences because they are tactile and creative, they engage the imagination, they appeal to the senses on many levels, and in them are stitched the hopes, dreams, and sometimes heartbreaks of their makers. Those emotions, captured in thread and fabric, are part of what make quilts different from other art forms.

In these QuiltPages the reader will discover how the artists have used their creativity to show anger at broken marriages; grief at the loss of a beloved friend or family member; strength as life circumstances change; courage as they see their children off to new and possibly dangerous adventures; delight in happy memories; and admiration of people they know from personal experience as well as figures from history and legend.

Three of the most moving of the Story QuiltPages include "A Frozen Moment", about the survival of a sister on September 11, 2001; "The Lone Woman of San Nicolas Island", a piece that retells a heartbreaking true story from the 1830s; and "Gone", about the loss of an infant granddaughter.

In the pieces found in this chapter, technique is often secondary to the tale that must be told, the story of the quilt.

The L. Elizabeth before her Sister Q. Mary

By all accounts this was Black Work; I a child and no Traitor.

The L. Elizabeth Prisoner in the Tower

Sandy Snowden

BRACKNELL, BERKSHIRE, ENGLAND • *March 2004*

"Part of my private textile journal of Elizabeth I, this QuiltPage was inspired by Tudor research for my costume work. It explores Elizabeth's imprisonment by her sister Mary in the Tower of London. Blackwork and silk damask form the background. The 'Scary Mary' face was printed on silk and overlaid on a period woodcut, an old necklace cross sewn over the candle on the table. Mary is often shown holding a cord with a book or medallion, so that became puppet strings leading to Elizabeth as a prisoner. My imaginary commentary may have been expressed by Elizabeth, who was fighting against entering Traitor's Gate lest she meet the same end as her mother, who was beheaded. Blackwork patterns from Mary Jane Collection are on linen; manipulated digital images were printed with an inkjet printer on silk. The woodcut images are from period sources at the British Library and were obtained from Lara E. Eakins at www.tudorhistory.org."

Judy Whitehead
CLEVELAND, NORTH CAROLINA

January 2006

"Every year in January I feel overwhelmed by year-end paperwork. Some years are worse than others; this year I felt like I had a filing cabinet dumping papers on my head continuously, and I was buried under paperwork. After several days of feeling like this, I had to translate my feelings into a quilt. Once I worked through this image, I felt refreshed and cheerfully tackled all the year-end paperwork. One of my intentions in this quilt was to concentrate on my proportion and free-motion quilting on my domestic machine. Both are areas I have had difficulty with. Overall, I am pleased with the end result."

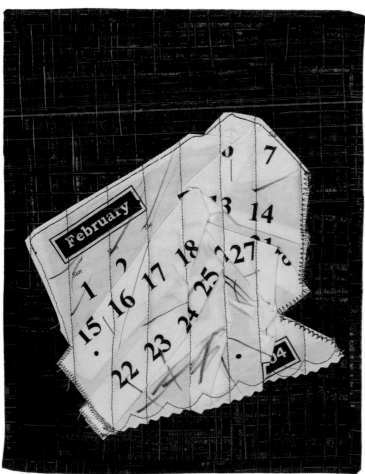

Alice McGunigle
SHIPPENVILLE, PENNSYLVANIA

February 2004

"February is always a bad month for me. It is the ugliest, bleakest, coldest time of the year here in Northern Pennsylvania. It is the month when furry, voracious, woodland creatures with tiny red eyes seek shelter from the cold in the recesses of my studio. It has also been a month when truly tragic things happen. In February 2002, my father died quite unexpectedly. Exactly two weeks later, the best dog I ever had died. Shortly after that my sister-in-law passed away. I decided to put February on notice. I printed the calendar page on fabric. I folded, mutilated, spindled, and even stapled it. And then I put it behind bars. I have had enough of February's nonsense."

Rachel Roggel
REHOVOT, ISRAEL

September 2003

"One Of A Kind"

"In 2003, my Journal Quilts were a button-charm series describing special people. The quilts use 435 one-of-a-kind buttons, out of the 80,000 I have collected over the last 10 years. For this QuiltPage, I honored Jewel Pearce Patterson. I have had this quilt in my mind ever since I met her in Houston. This quilt closes a circle. It's been 10 years since my first button quilt was exhibited at Quilt Expo IV in Karlsruhe, Germany. There, I ran into Karey Patterson Bresenhan, the director of Expo, who was enthusiastic about a new idea I had—creating a button-charm quilt. As busy as she was running the show, she had encouraging words, and later, my first button-charm quilt about Princess Diana was exhibited at the Grand Palais museum in Paris. This Journal QuiltPage is in honor of the woman (Mrs. Patterson) who forever changed my life through her daughter. I used organza, 49 one-of-a-kind buttons, letter beads, and hand quilting through the buttons."

February 2006

"MIA – Erinpura 1943"

"On May 1, 1943, German fighters attacked British Navy transport ships near Benghazi. In less than four minutes "Erinpura" sank with more than 1,000 soldiers aboard. The dead numbered 664, among them 140 Israeli volunteers to the British Army. On board was Jaacov Ben-Israel, who never returned home to his 12-year-old son, Uria. This quilt resembles a video game, but unlike in the game, the loss is real. It's inspired by the monument founded in Jerusalem Military Cemetery (1983). I sewed worry dolls, iridescent organza, Ellen Anne Eddy-dyed fabric, beads, and buttons. I made the quilt because as we all know, the third death is when no one is left to remember you."

Joanne M. Raab

"The Cruelest Month"

CLARKSON VALLEY, MISSOURI • *September 2002*

"On September 11, 2000, my father died. One year later, while on my way to visit his grave in New York, the twin towers were destroyed. It was hard to think of anything else that September, and now this anniversary is impossible to avoid. I painted Tyvek® strips that were woven and stitched and then distorted with a heat tool. It was a new technique for me that I found in SURFACES FOR STITCH by Gwen Hedley."

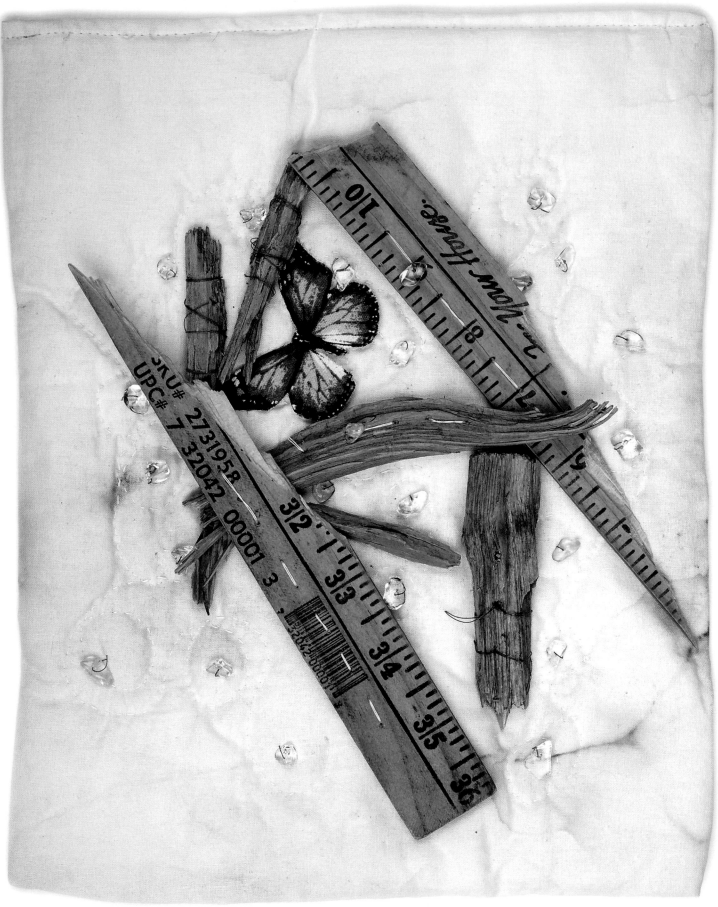

Lil Golston

THE WOODLANDS, TEXAS • *September 2005*

"This quilt helped me deal with my feelings about Hurricane Katrina. The butterfly is hope rising out of broken lives. The clear beads that were supposed to be raindrops turned out to be tears. I hand-dyed the fabric by burying it in mud for two weeks, hand-appliquéd found objects through drilled holes, fused, hand-beaded embellishments, and hand-quilted."

Patricia A. Montgomery
BROOKLYN, NEW YORK

March 2004

"In February 2004, after living in Oakland, California, for 25 years, I moved to Savannah, Georgia. As I explored this new location, this QuiltPage became a constant reminder of how important it is to believe in yourself and your dreams! My mixed-media collage was created using layers of threads, sheer ribbons, Angelina® fibers, and gold lamé on a hand-dyed fabric base covered with a golden sheer fabric and stamped with the word 'Believe.' I then machine-quilted the piece with computerized decorative stitches using rayon and metallic threads, and, finally, added stars, beads, and hot-fix crystals. This combination of materials creates the texture and iridescent effect."

Anne Harmon Datko
SILVER SPRING, MARYLAND

May 2004

"The Lone Woman of San Nicholas Island"

"This QuiltPage depicts the Gabrielino Indian woman who was abandoned on the outermost of the California Channel Islands in the 1830s. When her tribe was being removed by ship, she returned to shore to find her missing child and was left behind when weather forced the ship to sail without her. No attempt was made to rescue her or learn her fate. She survived on the bounty of the sea and the meager vegetation of the barren island. She made baskets to hold water and stitched dresses from cormorant skins. She never found her child. When she was rescued after some eighteen years, she had kept the skill of speech but had forgotten her language. She sang and danced and was a curiosity; she died from eating too much fruit only seven weeks after being rescued. Then the Fathers of the Mission baptized her and named her Juana Maria. Her story is told in Los Angeles, BIOGRAPHY OF A CITY by John and LaRee Caughey. Evening wear fabric, tulle, and fabric paint were used to create this piece."

Lynne Croswell
LUDLOW, VERMONT

March 2004

"Among the sewing items I found in Mom's sewing room (and later inherited), was her collection of more than 200 new and used zippers that included every color of the rainbow. The red zipper on the QuiltPage actually works and reveals a finished opening through to the back. I used a dismantled zipper for the binding."

February 2004

"Inheriting Mom's sewing room was at once a wonderful and a daunting event. My Journal Quilt chronicles the journey of sorting, using, and assimilating a cross section of her vast collection of notions and fabric. Mom sewed for all of her adult life—everything from clothing to home furnishings, dolls, and toys. She had nearly 500 metal covered-button forms in her collection. This piece includes almost half of them, which I covered using a variety of polka dot fabrics and colored Pigma® pens to change the color of many of the white dots."

Gloria Hansen

HIGHTSTOWN, NEW JERSEY • *September 2003*

"CAN Woman: Create Art Now"

"I wanted to create a woman with the words 'art' and 'create' intertwined. After experimenting, I decided to type the dictionary definition of 'art' and repeat it to create the background. I then drew the outline of a woman freehand and manipulated and colored it in Photoshop®. By changing the opacity of the woman, I was able to get the background words to show through. I added the words 'create, art, now' in a large font, resized them, set them at an angle, varied their opacity, and realized I had made an acronym! I am looking forward to making a larger CAN woman and using this design for note cards and/or fabric postcards. I used oil pastels and Caran D'Ache® crayons to enhance the image of the woman."

Heidi Stegehuis-Ihle

SOUTH LIMBURG, THE NETHERLANDS • *July 2005*

"Jason and the Argonauts"

"The King of Iolcus sent Jason, his son, on an impossible mission to find the Golden Fleece. Jason went with his friends on the ship Argo on his impossible journey. We all strive for impossible dreams, or the Golden Fleece, and for other better places. I used fusing with Vlisofix®, machine embroidery, free-motion quilting, and metallic fleece."

Kris A. Bishop
WOODBRIDGE, VIRGINIA

February 2002

"The Eagle Has Landed"

"My February QuiltPage explores the illusion of distance. I was inspired by the full moon that month and the 25th anniversary of the moon landing. After appliquéing the earth and the moon, thick metallic threads were couched on for the comet tail. Beads were added for the stars and the head of the comet."

Peggy Daley Spence
TULSA, OKLAHOMA

January 2006

"What a change from last year! Using some of the same fabrics seen in last year's piece, I created a mirror image of my 2005 January QuiltPage, made when I was a new widow and struggling with loss. I then re-interpreted the clump of trees on the way home from a new perspective. Improvisation from my heart created last year's image, a picture of loneliness and fear. I improvised again this year to create a portrait of my new January heart, filled with hope and joy. Life has moved on, and so have I. Grief is still there, as is winter. But hope and love have grown again."

Sidney Davis Jostes
NAPERVILLE, ILLINOIS

September 2003

"A Frozen Moment"

"This QuiltPage has special meaning
for me. On September 11, 2001, my
sister, Cathy Davis, was caught on the
63rd floor of the World Trade Tower II
when the first tower was hit. Paper
and debris were flying around outside
her window. She started down the
stairs, continuing even after being
passed by authorities telling everyone
to go back up. She made it to the
30th floor before United's Flight 175
slammed into that building at 9:03
a.m. She clung to the stairwell railings
as the building vibrated and then
continued on down, with uncommon,
everyday heroes around her all the
way. Unlike so many other people
that day, Cathy survived. I started
thinking about all those people and
their belongings that fell that day: like
Cathy's first pair of Manolo Blahnik
shoes, the pocket watch frozen at the
time the tower fell, a cell phone with
a last message on it, and an imaginary
letter. I created the kind of letter a
doomed mother might have left her
children. I wrote the letter on the
computer, printed it, scanned it, and
resized it to its very tiny size. The
miniature letter was printed onto silk
organza that was treated and ironed
to freezer paper, then fused to
more organza. This made it stiff
enough to be tucked and folded for
a three-dimensional effect. My
imaginary letter says:"

9/11/01

World Trade Center
New York, New York

Dear Todd, Sarah, and Samantha,

*I don't know if you'll get this letter. The
building's shaking and I'm trapped in a
stairwell, typing this on my laptop. When
you're about to die all you really care
about is telling the people you loved how
much you loved them. It doesn't matter
what kind of shoes you had or whether
you had the latest model car or the*
*largest house. We all go into the earth
the same way.*

*When I was 11 or 12, I can't remember
anymore, I loved the Beatles' music. I
still believe in the phrase, all you need is
love, love. Love is all you need.*

I love you.

Never forget.

Mom

Sidney Davis Jostes

NAPERVILLE, ILLINOIS

May 2003

"10 Things My Résumé Doesn't Tell You About Me"

"This quilt expresses my job-hunting frustration. I had difficulty getting an interview. I knew if an employer gave me a chance, I could prove valuable to them. The quilt text says: 'I am more than the words on my résumé reveal. I am a lover of Ed, my daughters Courtney and Ashley, books, coffee, chocolate, long walks on the beach, painting, photography, quilting, and snorkeling in the sea.' I printed my résumé onto treated fabric and jazzed it up with Setacolor paints. I wrote my message around the border of the text with black Pigma® pen. Working in Photoshop® I scanned objects like a bag of coffee, a bar of chocolate, a book I titled myself, and photos of my family and artwork; these I enhanced by manipulating the color saturation and contrast and re-sizing them. They were printed on fabric, cut out, and fused to white cotton. I placed them to correspond to the door openings I had cut in the résumé layer. The résumé was quilted to the image layer with invisible thread along the curved black line."

Anne Copeland

LOMITA, CALIFORNIA

January 2006

"My January QuiltPage is from a collaborative journal project by Jamie Fingal of Cut-Loose Quilters, a great art quilt group to which I belong. Our challenge for this month was to take a novel of our choice that was at least 150 pages long; we were to go to page 125 and select line 3—that was to be the theme of the quilt. My book was THE IMPROBABLE FUTURE by Alice Hoffman. I really stretched myself for this quilt. I used photo transfer for the words and the shadowy figure in the background as well as the rocky land. The woman, moon, and bird are actually paper and the whole is covered with netting to create an eerie feeling. Images of the shadowy figure and the woman in the right bottom were inspired by Quidam by Cirque du Soleil. The moon was cut from a larger picture of a planet taken by NASA and printed from the Internet."

She had seen this shadow the first day she met him but she hoped it would disappear.

Pamela Neiwirth

SILVER SPRING, MARYLAND

February 2006

"This was my first, very personal attempt to express in fabric the heartbreak of loving someone who has a drinking problem. The black-and-white checkerboard fabric on the sides represents the Indianapolis 500 race event, other car racing events, and the binges that ensue. Quilting has been a wonderful, creative outlet as I cope with the dissolution of the marriage."

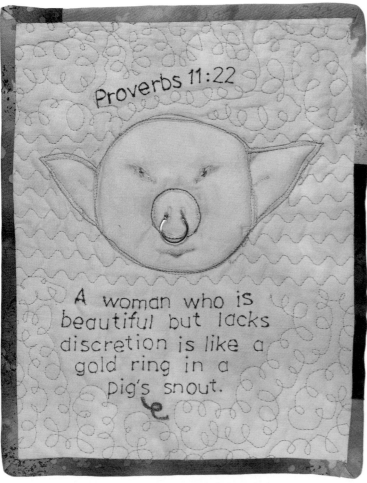

Cissy Wilson

RICHMOND, TEXAS

February 2006

"Pig's Snout"

"The imagery from the 'Book of Proverbs' in the NEW LIVING TESTAMENT is wonderful. 'Pig's Snout,' based on Proverbs 11:22, is a metaphor—likening a physical thing to a spiritual one. What fun to transform an idea into a picture! I used colored pencils to shade the pig's face and an earring whose mate was long lost. I also used hand-dyed fabric and did some trapunto."

Shawna Lampi-Legaree YELLOWKNIFE, NORTHWEST TERRITORIES, CANADA • *May 2005*

"Artist's Block"

"We had an active discussion about 'Artist's Block' on QuiltArt at one point. This is my version of what stops me from getting into my studio. I am pretty sure that most of us know that our extreme busyness really puts a damper on getting into our studios to create our life's work. I wrote all the words with Tsukineko® fabric ink and fused the shattered fabric on. I am not a fan of satin stitch, so I have been trying to find another method of ensuring that the pieces don't come off. I think I like this look of zigzagging back and forth three times over the edge."

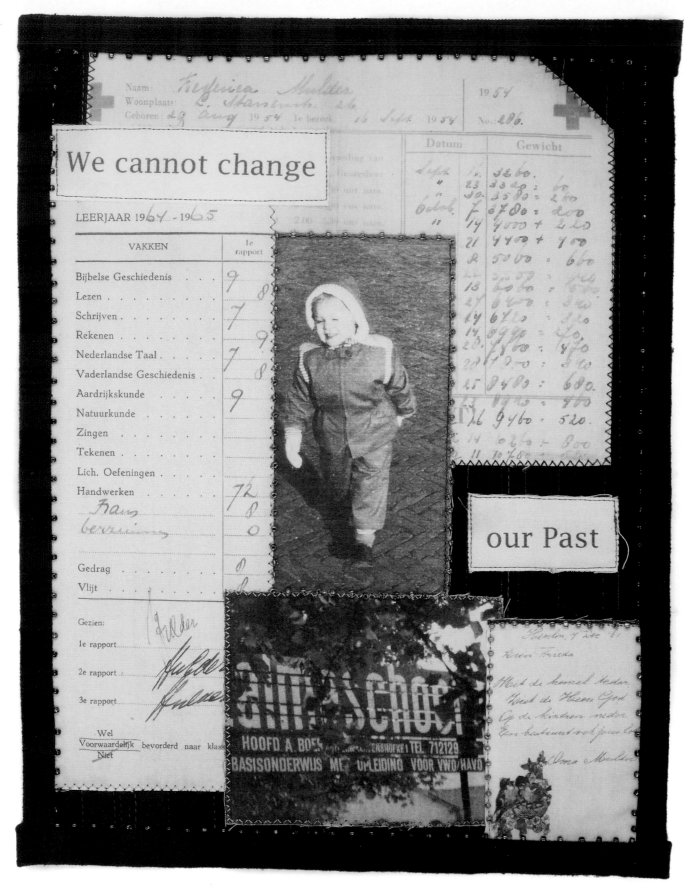

Frieda Oxenham

WEST LINTON, PEEBLESSHIRE, U.K. • *June 2005*

"What persuaded me to leave Holland and live in the U.K.? This decision, which proved to be life-changing, was made in a matter of seconds when I was picked up to go to my job interview at Heathrow and the radio happened to play 'Those Were the Days, My Friend' by Mary Hopkins. I made up my mind; I wanted no regrets later. All images were scanned into my computer and using Photoshop®, I changed their sizes to enable me to fit them onto my QuiltPage. I then printed them, as well as the text, onto fabric sheets from Color Textiles."

Rachel King Parris

BIRMINGHAM, ALABAMA

February 2006

"This little girl is my beloved sister-in-law who spent her childhood caring for three little brothers...two of whom were blind. She spends her adult life nurturing three brothers, an army officer husband, two sons, and two grandsons. I was inspired by Frances Holliday Alford who taught me art quilting 101 and Lesley Riley, whose QUILTED MEMORIES book inspired my use of family photographs."

Susan Elizabeth Slesinger

SEAL BEACH, CALIFORNIA

January 2006

"At my father's memorial services, I met Genia, his Swedish-Polish first cousin, for the first time. Genia related to me what her family had done to survive the Holocaust. In reviewing my father's photos, there are so many people pictured whose whereabouts are unknown—maybe some died in the camps, maybe others were shunned for possible collaboration with the Nazis? What happened in Wila, Switzerland, in the winter of 1930-31? Why did a Jewish boy have a photo of a snowman with a swastika? Did he build it? Did his friends make it? To create this piece, I used family photos from both my cousins and my family and photographs that I had taken. After determining which photos were of people who were from family lines that survived the Holocaust and which we could not identify or thought had perished, I scanned and enhanced them as little as possible to maximize the potential for seeing individuals (many photos, including group ones, were only passport-size). The oldest photo was a 19th-century family portrait taken in the family shop. The images were grouped and printed on pre-treated fabric backed with fusible web, then cut out. The machine embroidery was done before the photo collage was assembled."

Mimi Wohlberg

MERRICK, NEW YORK • *July 2003*

"Having a problem with my heel and hip in 2003 made me focus on where my feet were taking me each month of the year. In July we traveled to France and visited the U.S. military cemetery on the beaches of Normandy. That visit had a profound impact on my soul. Seeing the rows and rows of crosses and stars under a beautiful, peaceful, sunny sky was a moving and emotionally draining moment that led me to sit and shed tears. Using polymer clay for the crosses and stars was new to me; my tears needed to be included—they are foiled."

Ami Simms
FLINT, MICHIGAN

January 2006

"My mother has Alzheimer's. She is losing pieces of herself. Mom lived with us for nearly four-and-a-half years before she had to move into an Alzheimer's care facility this month. This QuiltPage was based on my sketch for the logo of the Alzheimer's Art Quilt Initiative, a project I created to raise awareness and fund research. I had to channel my grief into something positive. Although the quilt appears to be hand-pieced (at the top), it was entirely hand-appliquéd using techniques from my book, INVISIBLE APPLIQUÉ. Working from the right side, with a ladder stitch on marked sewing lines, intersections are far easier to match with this needle-turn technique."

Pamela Larsen
RENO, NEVADA

January 2005

"When starting my first journal page, I had begun a rough period in my life. As I poured my emotions into my quilt, I was able to release some of the bitterness that was living in my soul. After completing it, I thought I would burn it as a final purge, but I am glad I spared it. I worked with hand-dyed fabric and over-stamped with a hand-made stamp in two inks. I used Scrabble® tiles from a game I found at a thrift store to add necessary words to my piece."

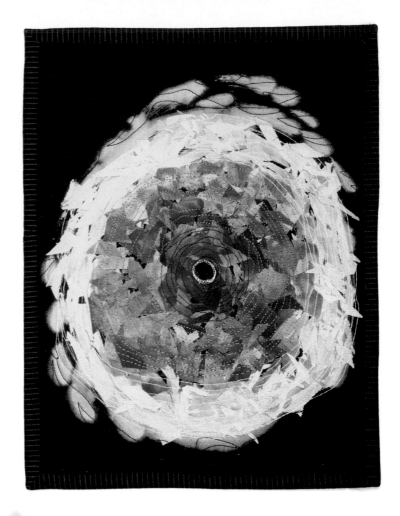

Mary Ann Littlejohn
HOUSTON, TEXAS

September 2005

"All of us on the Gulf Coast were glued to our televisions watching Hurricane Katrina approach, and we could see how large the 'eye of the storm' was. At our house, we were especially concerned, because although our son and his dog were already safe with us, their 100-year-old home in New Orleans was in danger. The image of the weather map is forever imprinted in my mind. Little did I know that we would be doing the same thing in Houston only a few weeks later, as we waited for Hurricane Rita. I used bleach discharge, fused appliqué, and free-motion quilting with neon yellow and orange thread to indicate movement around the hurricane's eye. This was my first experiment with a 'snippets' technique."

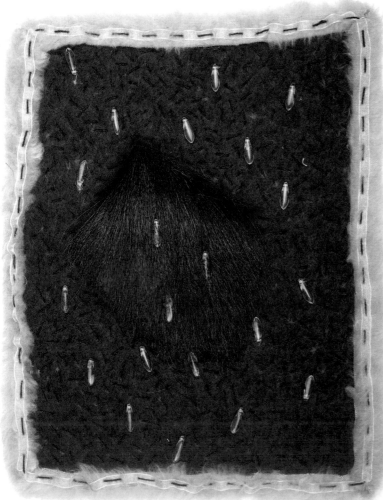

Christine Lussier
FORT WAYNE, INDIANA

May 2002

"Dear Heart"

"On July 3rd, 2001, at the tender age of 45, I had a heart attack. The journal quilts were an attempt to capture the healing process creatively. In May, my sweet old cat, Greystoke, was diagnosed with chronic renal failure, and a car hit my significant other, Tim. Lots of blood and tears, but the three of us drew comfort in just being together and healing. I fused layers of fleece and fake fur and added crystal beads for tears and a dyed deer tail."

Susan Kerr

UKIAH, CALIFORNIA • *July 2005*

"My precious baby granddaughter, Nefertiah, died on June 25th when a dresser in her parents' room fell on her, 10 days before her first birthday. Nothing I have ever experienced prepared me for such grief. When I was able, I made a tiny flannel quilt of triangles and turned it into a mourning quilt. The word 'gone' summed up my feelings a few weeks after her death..."

Linda McCurry

GILBERT, ARIZONA • *February 2005*

"Caged by Depression"

"My goal to devote more time and energy to art is being quashed by the nightmare of my day job. Dealing with an abusive boss and a scheming co-worker imprisons me in misery. I understand that my boss has a severe personality disorder, however, knowledge alone cannot dull the pain of his daily verbal assaults. What is going on with my co-worker? Is she simply following in the boss' psychopathic footsteps? Am I overreacting to her backstabbing because my self-esteem is under such heavy attack? I am baffled by her behavior. I have made every effort to treat her with kindness and respect, as a friend, but now it is clear that she intends to do me harm. I've got to get out of this poisonous environment and into a safe place. Why is this happening to me?"

"As a postscript, more than a year later, I have found a new job and great relief from the painful experience of my old job. My art and quilts and the support of my creative quilting friends helped me through this difficult period in my life. I am so thankful for their uncondi-tional acceptance and support."

Flowers, Plants, & Trees

The connection between people and flowers, plants, and trees is a strong one.

Perhaps it has to do with an innate sense of beauty that is satisfied only by nature and its bounty. Or maybe it has to do with color—the brilliance of scarlet tulips, the serenity of the myriad greens found in a forest, the gentle softness of delicate pastel flowers, even the scorching orange and black of forest fires.

Many of the quilt artists in this chapter have dealt with nature in small doses—one fern leaf magnified many times, one small segment of a multi-petal flower—while others have preferred to set their depiction of nature into perspective, placing the flower, tree, or leaf into a setting that shows off its details to perfection. Especially haunting are the winter scenes with the stark outlines of the trees cushioned in snow and ice, while the plant forms created with fractal software and threadwork bring floral art into the 21st century.

Some of the flowers and leaves exist only in the artist's imagination; others—in particular the ginkgo leaves, the fritillaria, and the persimmon— are near perfect copies of the actual plant. These artists indulged their imaginations and challenged their creativity with quilts that range from humorous to folk art to formal elegance.

Creative Quilting: THE JOURNAL QUILT PROJECT

Sarah Ann Smith

CAMDEN, MAINE
(This page and opposite)

January 2004 (Opposite)

"In January, we learned we would have to move away from our island home in Washington during 2004, so I needed a process that would let me participate in the Journal Quilt Project, but not take zillions of hours. I decided to play with photos taken on a rare snowy day on San Juan Island, transferred to cloth and intensely threadpainted for the series. Maggie Hunt's 2003 journals were a smaller picture 'framed' with fabric. I knew that the backdrops for the quilts at International Quilt Festival in Houston are black, so I thought that it would be fun to use a similar format. I decided to frame mine in black sateen to float the photos and lines of thread on the black backdrop, binding them in a batik fabric, and making the thread appear to float on the drapes between the central image and the binding. It worked!"

January 2006 (Top right)

"Color, as much as we all love it, is sometimes hard for quilters to understand and master. I wanted to make a series of small quilts illustrating different color principles for students to see the theory applied to cloth. This month, I tried to do an achromatic (black-white-gray, which is so not me!) piece, but ended up with a mostly monochromatic winter scene. Referring to several photos I had taken of the strong shadows in the Maine woods in winter, I composed the piece by fusing and layering the appliqués. I used light and dark shades of various neutral tones to create highlights and shadows on the tree trunks. I like quilts that, quite literally, break out of the box, so I let the trees and shadows extend beyond the boundaries of the QuiltPage."

February 2006 (Right)

"The bird of paradise, I realized, is the perfect illustration of the dual complementary color scheme: two sets of complementary colors—colors that are opposite each other on the color wheel. The blossom itself is vibrant orange and indigo blue, while the stem is green, edged in red. A piece doesn't come alive for me until I add the thread. After fusing the composition together, I marked the major leaf veins and shadows with chalk pencil, then free-motion quilted and threadpainted intensely. This way, I used my sewing machine needle and thread to vary the shade of the underlying fabric and create an illusion of depth, volume, light source, and shading. For the binding, I used camouflage-printed mesh, which creates a visual 'stop' at the edges, but allows the underlying color to peek through."

Terri Gavin
NEW YORK, NEW YORK

April 2004 (Left)

"This started as my class project in a workshop on hand painting with dyes by Hollis Chatelain. Lacking the time to decide what picture to work from, I grabbed my coffee table book of Georgia O'Keefe paintings. In this case, it was perfect, as she is one of my favorite artists and it was fascinating to try using one of her pictures. In addition, it made me slow down and concentrate on the details, which is something I need to do more often. The painted surface was covered in plastic to keep it from drying out for 24 hours so it could cure before being washed out. It was then machine-quilted."

Virginia O'Donnell
PORTLAND, OREGON

January 2006 (Bottom left)

"Three years ago I started taking watercolor classes, hoping that the skills I learned would enhance my work in fiber art. What I found out is that I see the whole world differently; my awareness of the things around me has changed significantly. I'm pleased that this piece shows my growth. I took a digital photo of my watercolor painting of a poppy, then printed the image on fabric and embellished the piece with free-motion quilting."

Carol Anne Clasper
LIVINGSTON, SCOTLAND

May 2004 (Opposite)

"I took a digital photograph of a fritillaria imperialis from my garden. I downloaded the photograph to Photoshop® and cropped it to get as clear a close-up as possible, leaving the background out of focus. Using temporary adhesive, I applied a piece of Habotai silk treated with Bubble Jet Set® to an overhead transparency. The transparency makes it easy to print onto fabric as it doesn't slip in the printer and has the added advantage of being reusable. I then free-motion quilted the flower using a variety of rayon threads. The stamens of the flower were accented with gold beads that were glued on."

Creative Quilting: THE JOURNAL QUILT PROJECT

Leslie Tucker Jenison
SAN ANTONIO, TEXAS

January 2006 (Opposite)

"Deconstruction #1"

"Part of an ongoing exploration using block deconstruction as a technique to explore print imagery, this QuiltPage features hand-dyed cotton that is pieced, discharged, screen-printed, then cut apart and reconstructed with more printing. It employs shibori and free-motion machine quilting."

May 2004 (Right)

"Digital Poppy"

"A response to discovering the first Oriental poppies of my spring garden, this QuiltPage is part of a continuing exploration combining digital media with stitching to enhance imagery. My digital photograph of the poppy was enlarged, scanned onto cotton, and fused with Pellon® WonderUnder®. Black cotton was bleach-discharged and the poppy fused to the fabric and then free-motion machine-embroidered and quilted."

Ann B. Graf
HOUSTON, TEXAS

February 2006 (Right)

"A daisy stamp I received as a gift was copied and enlarged to get the center image. I fused black fabric to both sides of a heavy interfacing and cut out the daisy with the idea of creating a shadowbox effect, although I wasn't sure how to achieve it. While experimenting, I used chunky beads as spacers and got the effect I was after, but how to attach it? Finally I decided to just glue it all in place."

Carolyn T. Abbott

BRAINERD, MINNESOTA

February 2006 (Top left)

"It's so cold and white outside that I long for spring. Red tulips are what I need. I cut them from hand-dyed fabric, use freeform piecing, and build up the composition on a design board, adding the green that I long for. I quilt the tulip's leaves, and the next thing I know, the weeds are starting to grow, too!"

Karen Williams

SEATTLE, WASHINGTON

April 2003 (Bottom left)

"Nobody sees a flower, really, it is so small.
We haven't time—and to see takes time like
to have a friend takes time."
— Georgia O'Keeffe

"Casting about for a theme, I was struck by some primroses blooming in my garden in January. My QuiltPages became my first garden journal, chronicling the succession of blooms outside my studio window. For my April quilt, I'd originally thought to focus on the tulips, but the calendula kept sneaking in, and eventually stole the show. I experimented with raw-edge fabric collage using fusible web, which worked beautifully for the calendula blossoms, as I was able to create their mop-headed splendor one petal at a time. In the background, more fusible showed than I wanted, so I added netting and long, textural hand stitches as camouflage. I stitched the collage to the quilt using a lopsided herringbone stitch. My biggest challenge in this piece was staying rough and chunky, as my work tends to be very neat and precise."

Linda Salitrynski

ROME, PENNSYLVANIA

May 2003 (Opposite)

"The flowers are here! This quilt was made from torn commercial and hand-dyed fabric strips, some placed flat and others twisted, that were then stitched down. The center of the flower consists of a pile of threads with a piece of fuchsia tulle over the top to contain the threads. The quilt is machine-quilted with rayon thread."

Creative Quilting: THE JOURNAL QUILT PROJECT

Helen Cowans

WOOLER, NORTHUMBERLAND, U.K.

January 2006 (Opposite)

"The Green Man is a common image and led me to think about a Green Goddess and Mother Earth. This QuiltPage is one interpretation. The Goddess of Life—of nature, of the trees, and of plants growing from and of the earth—features red symbols on her body inspired by carved rocks found locally that date from many thousands of years ago. Techniques used include Kantha-style quilting and beading."

February 2006 (Top right)

"February's QuiltPage carries on my theme of the Goddess and Mother Earth, a topic that fascinates me. It features some of my favorite materials: metal, organza, and vibrant hand-dyed silk velvet. I used embossed, heated, and painted copper shim according to a technique in PAPER, METAL & STITCH by Maggie Grey and Jane Wild; this technique causes the paints to speckle and merge."

Janis Bennett-Salcfas

ELIZABETH LAKE, CALIFORNIA

July 2005 (Right)

"This QuiltPage was an experiment in techniques and individuality. I wanted to do something different from anything else I have ever done. I cut scraps of a pretty hand-dyed fabric and let them drop onto a piece of WonderUnder®, pressing to secure them. I drew a tree on two sheets of Sulky® Solvy™ and threadpainted to create the tree, then layered and quilted the piece, attaching the tree and all of the beads by hand."

Creative Quilting: THE JOURNAL QUILT PROJECT

Kathy York
AUSTIN, TEXAS

March 2003 (Opposite)

"Michael's Flower"

"I was so inspired by Lisa Harvey's QuiltPage 'Talk to the Hand'. I wanted to try something simple, so I selected the same flower that has been recurring in my art since high school. I faced many challenges with this piece and ultimately spent the entire month making this little quilt. I enjoyed playing with D'UVA™ Chroma Coal® pastels, large seed quilting stitches, and my first attempt at embellishing with beads. And I loved the final result!"

Beth Ober
DAMASCUS, MARYLAND

March 2005 (Top right)

"To me, March is synonymous with the end of winter— at last! I felt compelled to depict my sense of the earth awakening from the cold winter months with tendrils of green reaching upward into bold colors. This month was another 'playing with fabric paints' adventure using various types and brands of paints to create the background, vine, and other details. While the paint was still wet, I sprinkled coarse salt over the fabric; as the paint dried it created an interesting textural pattern. Then I added the vine, leaves, and details by hand-painting them onto the background with assorted Jacquard® textile paints."

Terri H. Winsauer
DAYTON, TEXAS

January 2006 (Right)

"I decided to base my QuiltPages on different episodes of 'Simply Quilts.' I tape or watch it daily and always learn something new. I think, 'I would like to try that,' and then I never get the chance. Well, that is what's so wonderful about having the Journal Quilt Project! My first QuiltPage was made with techniques learned from fuser Laura Wasilowski. I have a new machine and it also gave me a chance to play. For this, I fused raw-edge appliqué and 100 percent cottons, then machine-quilted."

Vivien Zepf
THORNWOOD, NEW YORK

August 2004 (Top left)

"Inspired by the gardens around the house and a book of Pat Sloan designs, I created my own flower arrangement. I've never made any folk art-style quilts before, so this was fun. It was a personal challenge to find a fitting place for the snowflake in the design (since I had tasked myself with including a snowflake in each QuiltPage). I embellished this with as many beads as I could to add dimension."

Magda Stryk Therrien
KANATA, ONTARIO, CANADA

June 2004 (Bottom left)

"This piece was a work of joy and frustration. The process of freeform hand beading was a very time-consuming, occasionally overwhelming, reflective, and joyful task. As I finished each portion of the tree, it took courage to go on, as I was sure that whatever I did next would ruin what I already loved about the piece. In the end I was thrilled with the radiant beauty and felt that it truly was my personal tree of life."

Kelly Monroe
REDWOOD CITY, CALIFORNIA

January 2003 (Opposite)

"Two Feet & A Heartbeat"

"In January, my husband was diagnosed with a sky-high cholesterol count and insulin resistance. That triggered a new way of eating and exercise. Our young daughter's footprints represent both the future and much-needed exercise. Inspired by the quilt's title, symbols of health and exercise—the carrots and footprints—were hand-painted and raw-edge appliquéd. The heartbeat was silk-screened. I rummaged through our pantry tearing off labels from the newly forbidden foods for the border and binding. Beading added dimension and detail to the finished piece."

YOU ARE WHAT YOU EAT

CHAPTER 3: FLOWERS, PLANTS, & TREES

Creative Quilting: THE JOURNAL QUILT PROJECT

Frieda Oxenham

WEST LINTON, PEEBLESSHIRE, U.K.

June 2004 (Opposite)

"I love to let foxgloves self-seed around my garden in Scotland. I like their spots and the way the bumblebees sneak inside. Foxgloves have many exquisite color combinations, but here I have introduced a few of my own that nature hasn't gotten around to yet. I scanned my photograph of the foxglove into the computer and changed the color, using both the original and the altered color version to make what is a nod to a Nine-Patch quilt layout. As the foliage is also beautiful, I used machine couching with green bouclé knitting yarn so the flowers look like they are nestled in greenery."

Sue Andrus

TOWANDA, PENNSYLVANIA

September 2004 (Top right)

"I found sun printing, using flowers and leaves on a painted cotton fabric, to be much-needed therapy. This fern sun print was cut apart to represent my life falling apart. The pieces were appliquéd in a more orderly manner than previous QuiltPages for this year, to show some pieces of my life coming back together. This is a more calming quilt to look at than my frayed and scattered QuiltPages of July and August. The book SKYDYES by Mickey Lawler was my initial inspiration for trying fabric painting and sun printing."

Anna M. Rice

TAMPA, FLORIDA

January 2006 (Right)

"I am a fractal artist. Fractal geometry allows us to see the unseen, as the shape of everything in nature is a fractal. When I rendered this particular fractal, I thought of a tropical flower blooming in the cold of winter. Using Tierazon software, I rendered a revised geometric equation to create this fractal image, manipulated the color saturation electronically, and changed the size of the image; I then inkjet-printed it onto silk. To keep the focus on the fractal image, I used metallic thread to enhance and outline-quilt it. The backing used for this piece is also a fractal I created by capturing the color gradients used in the fractal image, rendering and printing the color fractal on silk."

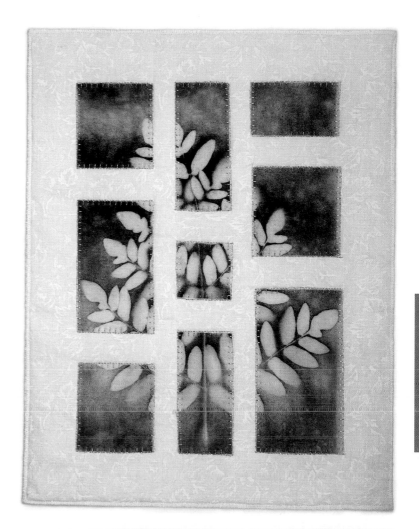

Norma Schlager

DANBURY, CONNECTICUT • February 2006

"Paint Chips"

"For a color theory class, I had previously used those little samples you pick up at the paint store and had decided that they were too special to throw away. When I discovered that they could be sewn through, I knew they would go on quilts. Several paint chips of the same or similar color were placed side-by-side, fused to WonderUnder®, then cut into tiny pieces and fused two or three at a time to a Teflon® pressing sheet, following the drawing of the tree on paper beneath the pressing sheet. When finished, the whole tree was fused to the background fabric. I used release paper on top of the chips while fusing, or the heat of the iron would have melted the paint. Leaves and flowers in the grass were added one at a time. Quilting through the paper made noticeable holes, so I quilted around the chips, except for the area in the grass. If you look carefully, you can read the names of some of the paint colors."

Norma Schlager

DANBURY, CONNECTICUT • *May 2004*

"I had dyed more than 25 yards of fabric several months earlier trying to find the perfect blue. I never did get quite the shade I was looking for but did acquire a great blue stash. This is a small sample. I machine-embroidered the leaves with a variegated rayon thread."

Creative Quilting: THE JOURNAL QUILT PROJECT

Katharine Stubbs Ward

RIVIERA BEACH, FLORIDA

January 2006 (Opposite)

"My Journal Quilt for 2006 will feature the same palm tree, using a different technique each month. Pastels were used to draw this shape and then colors were blended using fingertips and a paper towel. The pastels were set with hairspray. Three coats were applied, spraying lightly and allowing each application to dry completely before spraying again. A lot of threadpainting was used to shape and accent details, and the piece was set with a hot, dry iron."

Els Vereycken

HASSELT, BELGIUM

March 2005 (Top right)

"The weather is warming up. The buds are coming open. Trees are coming into leaf. Each leaf is growing and extending its surface. My own digital photographs are the origins of my paper and hand-dyed fabric cutouts. I accented the leaves with quilting stitches of different colors."

patsy monk *(sic)*

WIMAUMA, FLORIDA

January 2006 (Right)

"Looks Like Arizona To Me"

"As we drove from Florida to California in January, the scenery took a radical change when we left civilization for the desert part of the trip through Arizona. The most dramatic feature was huge Saguaro cacti. They defy drought to live in hot, barren earth. Many of these majestic plants are more than 100 years old. Only the hardiest survive and grow slowly. This left me with the motto: 'Be determined to survive and grow, regardless of the circumstances.' The landscape and sky are raw-edge appliqué strips; clouds are torn pieces of batting, machine-stitched in place. Bobbin threadpainting blended and softened the edges of the strips, and green yarns were crocheted in a chain for the cactus, then hand-stitched to an original drawing. Piping was a new technique for me this year."

Franki Kohler

OAKLAND, CALIFORNIA • *January 2006*

"During the fall of 2004, a fierce windstorm caused the center third of my heavily fruit-laden Fuyu persimmon tree to collapse. I wasn't sure the tree would survive, but it did, bearing a small crop of fruit in 2005. I simply had to celebrate its survival. My QuiltPage uses photo transfer and free-motion embroidery to threadpaint the fruit and branch onto cotton fabric."

Carol Ruth Brydon Koford

ANCHORAGE, ALASKA • *January 2005*

"We moved to Alaska last month and have become very aware of the light, the dark, the sky, and the position of the sun. I had to capture the entrancing colors in the sky as I saw them through the stands of bare trees, so I sketched the trees to capture their silhouettes. I painted sheets of cloth and came up with the colors I was seeing, using beads to represent the hoarfrost."

Creative Quilting: THE JOURNAL QUILT PROJECT

Claire Anne Gabrielsen Teagan

HIGHLAND, MICHIGAN

January 2004 (Opposite)

"I wanted to try out some of the inks, paints, and dyes that I had bought at International Quilt Festival in Houston before I bought new things at the spring Festival in Chicago! This QuiltPage features different hand-dyed silks with leaves painted and stamped onto the fabrics. Fresh leaves were used to print with paints onto the fabrics. A stamp of foiling glue and car detailing foil was used for the fern leaves, and free-motion quilting outlines the stamped leaves."

Carol Soderlund

GENEVA, NEW YORK

August 2003 (Top right)

"A number of my journal pieces have used leaves; they are such universal symbols of growth and change and so inspiring in their intricacies of shape and color. It is only August, yet already I have found a bronzed oak leaf, a reminder of the fleeting warmth of summer. I used sun printing with Setacolor paint, grasses, and leaves for the background fabric, and sponged metallic copper fabric paint on the back side of an oak leaf, pressing it onto black fabric to create the bronzed leaf image. After machine embroidering and carefully trimming the leaf, I arranged it, along with slivers of fusible black organza, and fused it in place. I free-motion quilted the piece, and stitched the leaf in place, anchoring it along its stem only, so that it would be somewhat dimensional."

Jane Hall

RALEIGH, NORTH CAROLINA

September 2004 (Right)

"Using a branch from my Japanese red maple tree as a pattern, I cut leaves from several batiks and hand-dyed fabrics, arranged them in a cluster, and fused them to a background. The leaf veins were free-motion stitched and, after outlining the shapes, the open spaces were filled with small stipple quilting. The binding is pieced using some of the leaf fabrics."

Marci Hainkel

KANSAS CITY, MISSOURI

February 2006 (Top left)

"I've always enjoyed looking at trees, especially to see the contrast between the branches and the sky. This year I based each QuiltPage on a tree I'd seen that month, which has had the added benefit of reminding me to stop and enjoy the trees instead of rushing by. I used fabric fusing and free-motion machine embroidery, a new adventure for me this year."

Kathleen Caron Molatch

EASTBROOK, MAINE

January 2006 (Left)

"Lonesome"

"There are trees all through my psyche, metaphors for parts of life. January's tree has grown strong, sturdy enough to stand the lonely month and its cold gray days. This year we had no snow, so the tree braves an empty landscape unsoftened by a blanket of white. I started the tree with wool roving, which looked wonderfully gnarled, but I couldn't keep it in place. So, I threadpainted heavily over the wool to create the bark texture and thus affixed the wool to the background. The wool's fuzzy edges add an unexpected backlight to the tree."

Sherry Boram

PENDLETON, INDIANA

June 2003 (Opposite)

"Forest Stump"

"This drawing is my first attempt at using an AirPen® while in a class with Susan Shie. I later painted it with thinned Setacolor and quilted it with Susan's distinctive chicken stitches, using rayon and metallic threads. The meditative nature of hand stitching let me absorb these new techniques while wondering where they would take me!"

Creative Quilting: THE JOURNAL QUILT PROJECT

Jeanne M. Marklin

SILVER SPRING, MARYLAND

February 2006 (Opposite)

"February Promise"

"I have been adding silk to my pieces, and in this piece I liked the matte quality of the paint against the luster of the silk, which has been stamped with fabric paint, fused, and machine-quilted."

Cherry Jackson

YARRAVILLE, VICTORIA, AUSTRALIA

June 2002 (Top right)

"Regrowth: Everything Old is New Again"

"June in Australia is wintertime, when all the deciduous trees are bare of leaves and blossoms. I love looking at the tree skeletons and shapes so I decided to depict June in an abstract fashion. The ideas of 'everything old is new again' and 'rebirth and regrowth' are common themes in my quilts. I want to respond to my environment through my art and music. I used furnishing fabrics and materials from my stash, along with commercial wool and wools that I had space-dyed by spreading the wool out in a container of water and dripping dye onto it in irregular intervals. This allowed the colors to run and blend, creating new colors and a random, non-repeating design. Used CDs were sewn to the background and organza strips were added to the border for extra dimension."

Alexandra Claire Tsubota

TORRANCE, CALIFORNIA

January 2004 (Right)

"I joined the Journal Quilt Project to push myself out of my comfort zone and try new things. For January, my goal was to try working intuitively. I began with a set of blue fabrics that I cut and sewed randomly until I had a background I liked. The burgundy fabric was added next, using reverse appliqué and some decorative stitching. It was awful and couldn't be undone because I had cut the background, so it sat in a corner until the deadline. At that point I forced myself to just do something to finish it and really surprised myself—I ended up liking the final result! (You can hardly see the burgundy!)"

Jackie L. Mauer

WARREN, TEXAS

May 2003 (Left)

"This tree was inspired by Caryl Bryer Fallert's 'Dancing Tree.' Like each soul, each tree has its own personality, its own interpretation. All are swayed by changes in life. At times we feel barren and alone. Other times, we feel free and actually do dance with the winds of life. Hand-painted fabric is enhanced with pearlescent paints, batik fabric, metallic and rayon threads, and raw-edge reverse appliqué."

Martha Kleihege

SAN FRANCISCO, CALIFORNIA

January 2004 (Bottom left)

"It was a cold, wet, wintry day in San Francisco, the wind blowing the thick fog so that it was difficult to see across the street. As I walked past the plum tree outside my front door, I noticed that there were a few pink blossoms opening up and my day brightened, knowing that spring was on its way. With the plum tree as my inspiration, I tried threadpainting freehand with my sewing machine for the first time."

Linda S. Schmidt

DUBLIN, CALIFORNIA

July 2004 (Opposite)

"I continue to experiment with the possibilities of puff paint, Fiber Etch®, and cracked ice. Here I pared my earth element down to the essentials—water, rock, sky, and tree—based on a mental picture of the bare, rocky environment of Yosemite. The tree was simply squirted out of a puff paint tube, left to dry, then puffed up with a heat gun, and painted with fabric paints, Shiva® Paintstiks®, and Jacquard® metallic paint powders. The rocks were made the same way, but with the addition of mica chips. The water is melted iridescent cracked ice over blue water fabric. The leaves were made with a new process I devised. First I took a tree-leaf batik fabric onto which I squirted Fiber Etch®, waited for it to dry, heated the fabric with an iron, pinned it upside down to parchment paper, and then soaked it in water until the blackened Fiber Etch® dissolved and floated away. Then I dried it with my iron, laid it on top of Steam-A-Seam II Lite®, and fused it. I turned it over and fused it again, then pulled off the release paper, which gave me clumps of leaves that could then be fused to the background to create the illusion of leaves. Everything was then sewn to a background of Totally Stable™ with an invisible zigzag stitch, the background was removed, and the piece quilted."

Creative Quilting: THE JOURNAL QUILT PROJECT

Cynthia Paugh St. Charles
BILLINGS, MONTANA

January 2004 (Opposite)

"Last summer our state was aflame with forest fires. While driving along the highway one July evening, we passed very close to a raging firestorm. The image of the trees silhouetted against the flames at night remained with me into the chilly month of January, when I pulled out a piece of my hand-dyed fabric and tried to convey that image for my first QuiltPage of the new year. I used a reverse-appliqué method learned in a workshop taught by David Walker."

Kathie Briggs
CHARLEVOIX, MICHIGAN

January 2005 (Top right)

"I live in the woods, and the trees provide inspiration in all seasons. For this QuiltPage, I painted both sides of a large piece of Tyvek® with several shades of brown acrylic paint, then cut oversized rectangles for the tree trunks and branches. I used a heat gun to melt and shape the Tyvek®, and then stitched the tree to the pieced background. Angelina® fibers were first heat-fused, then free-motion machine stitched over the scene."

Margreta K. Silverstone
TAKOMA PARK, MARYLAND

June 2003 (Right)

"I liked the branch I made for my April QuiltPage and used it as the basis for the trunks of trees for a few months. This month, I played with foil transfer appliqué. One attempt produced a mess on my iron. Another attempt turned out fine. How do I complete the image? When does a tree trunk look like this? Everything shimmers under moonlight. I decided to play with holographic thread and sequins, too."

Chris Hoover

SAINT CLOUD, MINNESOTA • *July 2005*

"It's been a hot, dry July—even the breeze is warm—so I tried to convey the sound of parched leaves rustling outside a window using Angelina® fibers, Sliver™ thread, and foil. Fabric for the window was pleated first, then foil transfer adhesive was applied and dried, and the foil transferred to the fabric. The window was reverse-appliquéd to the background, leaves were added, and Sliver™ thread was used to quilt and accent lines in the batik fabric."

Animals & Insects

    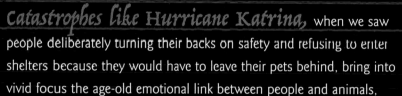

Catastrophes like Hurricane Katrina, when we saw people deliberately turning their backs on safety and refusing to enter shelters because they would have to leave their pets behind, bring into vivid focus the age-old emotional link between people and animals, making the undeniable point that to many people, their pets are their family.

The QuiltPages in this chapter not only reflect the appeal that animals have held for artists throughout the centuries—as shown in the multitude of important art exhibitions, commissions, and art books based on animals, but they also show the deep, abiding love and strong appreciation that many of the artists have for the animals they depict in their work. Many different techniques have been used to capture the character of these animals and also, sometimes, to tell their stories. The QuiltPages in this chapter celebrate dogs, cats, fish, birds and their feathers, horses, farm animals, insects such as butterflies and moths, wild animals, and even imaginary animals. Whether the artists are picturing beloved pets or extraordinary creatures that they have known, heard about, or seen in nature, their respect for the spirit of the animal shines through and is an integral part of these images.

Nancy Sterett Martin

OWENSBORO, KENTUCKY • April 2005

"I have always admired the works of Annemieke Mein. After reading her book THE ART OF ANNEMIEKE MEIN, WILDLIFE ARTIST IN TEXTILES and studying her techniques, I decided to experiment with some of them. I have done a lot of free-motion sewing, but the challenge for me was the bird's nest. When it was finished, I was pleased with it."

Vivien Zepf
THORNWOOD, NEW YORK
January 2006

"I've decided to create QuiltPages based on photographs of places and things we've seen on vacation. For January, I recreated a picture of an unknown bird we saw in Costa Rica. I've never made anything based on a photo before nor anything that was supposed to look realistic. I struggled with every decision. This was a challenge for me, but I like the end result, which used raw-edge appliqué and embellishment, enough to try something like this again."

Sandra Betts
ST. JOHN, NEW BRUNSWICK, CANADA
May 2002

"The robins have returned and are industriously building their nests. This one decided to build in a tree outside my window, so I could watch its daily progress. In the course of time, two beautiful blue eggs appeared at two different times, but they could not withstand the attacks of some aggressive grackles. The empty nest signifies the failure of the female to raise her young but stands as a memento of her hard work. During the progress of these events, I decided to honor the robin's perseverance and industry by making it my May QuiltPage. I have had surgery on my hands and have not been able to do hand needlework for several years. May was the month for me to persevere and try hand appliqué and trapunto."

Katharine Stubbs Ward

RIVIERA BEACH, FLORIDA • *January 2005*

"My goal for this year is to work with the fabric as printed, and make as much use of that as possible to create my QuiltPages. This silhouette of a great blue heron was created with black fabric and fused to a batik background. By careful placement and cutting, the colors needed no additional paint or thread work to create an evening effect. Feathers were accented with thread."

Katharine Stubbs Ward

RIVIERA BEACH, FLORIDA • *June 2005*

"Wood storks gather at sunset in large, noisy congregations in the swamp, perching on impossibly thin tree limbs. South Florida has built over and contaminated great areas of their nesting sites, so they are moving out of our state! My background fabric is 100 percent upholstery fabric that has been painted with textile paint to give that sunset glow over the swamp. Threadpainting is used to give detail to the bird."

Linda S. Schmidt

DUBLIN, CALIFORNIA • *January 2006*

"The Eagle Has Landed"

"I was gifted with a free, five-day trip to Art Quilt Tahoe and elected to take Hollis Chatelain's dye painting class. I used as a basis the photo my brother, John Evanick, took of an eagle flying to his handler. I learned a lot about quilting and thread, contour, line, and design. I also learned to 'Suck it up, Princess,' once it really hit me that dye painting is not the same as fabric painting. What you see is not what you get! I traced the enlarged photo onto prepared fabric with a Pigma® marker, then mixed up PRO Print Paste Mix and stirred Procion® dyes into them. I painted on the fabric with these dyes, let it dry, then had to wash it out nine times using Synthrapol to get rid of the excess dye before quilting."

Joy F. Palmer

SAN JOSE, CALIFORNIA • *March 2004*

"I have recently relocated my sewing table so that I look out at the birds visiting our bird feeder...it is much better looking at birds and listening to the TV or radio while I quilt! I drew the bird with colored pencils on muslin and then threadpainted away. Rummaging around in my fabrics for something suitable for a background, I found the scrap that I had used as a blotter while painting some fabric and decided that it would make a great background. I appliquéd the bird to the fabric and drew a few branches in with markers and colored pencils, using the branch outlines and the bird as my quilting lines. Leftover scraps of Timtex™ were lying around on the floor near my sewing table, so in the spirit of trying new things, it became my 'batting.' I've decided that small works intended for the wall instead of the bed don't always need a traditional binding—a little fusing, a little glue, and it's done!"

Kathie Briggs
CHARLEVOIX, MICHIGAN

February 2006

"Suddenly the trees were covered with cedar waxwings. Dozens of birds hopped from branch to branch devouring the winterberries. In a single movement, the flock left one tree only to land in the next. In minutes, the birds and the berries were gone, but for an instant they brightened a February morning."

Joanne M. Raab
CLARKSON VALLEY, MISSOURI

August 2002

> *"Oh what can ail thee, wretched wight,*
> *alone and palely loitering;*
> *The sedge is withered from the lake,*
> *and no birds sing."*— Keats

"Dead crows, ducks, and migratory birds were appearing all over the Midwest. As a lifelong birdwatcher I was worried that the West Nile virus would damage much of the bird population. Poor birds."

Frances Caple

ISLE OF LEWIS, SCOTLAND • *April 2005*

"Feathers"

"At college, we had a three-day, screen-printing class with Kim McCormack, and I used two of the pieces as my March and April QuiltPages. April is a devoré feather design, and the screen was made using a real feather. I added more detail with hand embroidery, then feather-quilted the negative space around the feather."

Creative Quilting: THE JOURNAL QUILT PROJECT

Mary Ellen Heus

WAUKESHA, WISCONSIN

March 2005

"My QuiltPage goal was to use a different material each month to depict a design based on the life cycle of moths. In March, my material was threadpainting on water-soluble plastic. While I find some repetitive work to be calming and meditative, this work left me agitated and impatient; I found I could not 'paint' for long stretches of time. The design is based on a photograph by Paul Starosta in BUTTERFLIES AND MOTHS."

Della Alice Cruz *(Opposite)* **OMAHA, NEBRASKA** • *August 2004*

"Almost every day, my dog Casey and I walk a trail which meanders alongside a small creek. One day I saw a large ball of white fly across the trail in front of me, into the trees. I heard a mewing sound. My subconscious translated what I had seen: something was thrown and hit and injured a small animal. I reached out and pulled aside a tree branch that was blocking my view. There was a hawk, wings still spread, holding a rabbit...a huge hawk, frozen against the ground. The rabbit mewed again. I looked at the hawk, my mind registering the almost four-foot wingspan and the head the size of a tennis ball. I froze. Casey, at my side, was also frozen. The hawk pulled its wings in, still holding the rabbit. I stood without moving for about 30 seconds, watching the hawk watch me. I released the branch and stepped slowly back from the trees. The hawk released the rabbit, which darted across the path at my feet. The hawk flew up to a low branch. I could see him clearly now, and we watched each other for a while. I apologized for ruining his dinner and continued my walk, hoping the hawk would hunt successfully again that day.

"I've stopped and looked at the site several times. There is no sign of the hawk or the rabbit or my encounter with them. All through the month, I found and picked up feathers along the path. My 'collection' became this QuiltPage."

Lily M. Kerns

MARIONVILLE, MISSOURI • *September 2002*

"My husband's Parkinson's disease has left him completely helpless now, but he can still joke with his nurses and argue with me. His 'Mr. Fix-it' instincts are still intact, which is what we argue about. We are still waiting for the next chapter of our lives, but we are content. I wonder why I wrote that last phrase, but realize it is true. This is another of my transition quilts. The batik I used for my previous quilts was the inspiration for the threadpainting, which I had never done before. This one felt unfinished until I added the butterfly. I think I must do more of these, for 'When we see death, God sees butterflies!'"

Mary Jane Hoag

LAS VEGAS, NEVADA • *August 2005*

"While focusing on the wildflowers of the Southwest, I saw the Chamisa shrub in full bloom with swarms of butterflies hovering above, and it was a Kodak moment for me. My goal was to capture that moment using yarns, flosses, and fabrics, along with hand-painted butterflies."

Marie E. Johansen

FRIDAY HARBOR, WASHINGTON • *January 2006*

"Chellie Bee"

"Chellie (aka Chelliebee the Beast) was the apple of my eye. Although she was not always a perfectly well-mannered kitty, she made me laugh every day. I became embarrassingly hysterical when she died unexpectedly at a young 12 years. She took a piece of my heart that day. I still miss her. Our pets become our family...with all of the 'for better or for worse' that loving them can sometimes entail!"

Marie E. Johansen

FRIDAY HARBOR, WASHINGTON • *February 2006*

"Odie"

"Odie has been with me for 17 years. He demands a daily dose of Vitamin E, and he still plays like a kitten. He is, I believe, an old soul, always caring for his family—those with two legs as well as four. He is the one that the others go to for comfort. He is kind and gentle and everything good that four paws can be! If I could clone one thing only, it would be Odie."

Margaret Hunt
"Pete"

CLARKS HILL, SOUTH CAROLINA • *May 2004*

"Pete is a wonderful mutt from the pound that my son Drew's fiancée, Emily, adopted. He is such a sweetie, and he looks a lot like Tramp in 'Lady and the Tramp', except he is darker. Pete likes nothing better than a good romp in the river or in the lagoons in our neighborhood. Pete started out as a raw-edge appliqué collage but he was not doing well, so I started threadpainting him with a variety of threads...and that was what brought him to life."

Jean Myers Boos
CADES, SOUTH CAROLINA

August 2003

"Hot weather left me sluggish and my ambition low. To keep my theme of 'Making Time,' I cut and fused printed dogs to my hourglass shape, then couched chenille 'fur' around it and the outside edge of the quilt. 'Like Sands Through the Hourglass, So Are the Dog Days of Our Lives' proves that whimsy and creativity can surface, even on days when you don't want to make the effort."

Sue Wilson
FLAGSTAFF, ARIZONA

April 2005

"This is Domino, a bearded collie, and the best friend a gal ever had. This QuiltPage was created using Sue Olsen's pattern and technique. It's a fast and fun fusing technique with edges butted against each other rather than overlapped. I adapted the pattern for my use (focused on the face, changed the coloring to match Domino's, added embellishments). Then I decided to cover the entire top with a layer of tulle before I free-motion stitched around the pieces and added a few beads in the flowers."

Linda Hall

DOUGLASSVILLE, PENNSYLVANIA • *March 2004*

"Painted Ponies"

"I experimented with satin stitch and couched black yarn for a more three-dimensional effect to make the piece look like a real stained glass window. The horses were cut out of printed fabric and fused onto the background before the satin stitching was applied. I used Madeira® black core metallic thread and am pleased with the stained glass look this gave to the piece. It gave me the courage to try a real Tiffany window pattern in the future."

Linda Hall

DOUGLASSVILLE, PENNSYLVANIA

February 2004

"Kessler Highlands"

"I was inspired by a photograph of the Yorkshire Dales, U.K., from the book JAMES HERRIOT'S YORKSHIRE, and used it as a guideline for the background landscape, with its hedgerows and sheep fields. Gail Kessler of Ladyfingers Sewing Studio designs fabric for Andover Fabrics™, and I used cutouts from her sheep fabric as the foundation for the sheep. I incorporated unspun, shredded lambswool in two colors on the bodies of the sheep and stitched the wool to the background with a narrow but open zigzag stitch before starting to threadpaint. I discovered that thread-painting faces is challenging and delicate work. It took four experiments with the sheep to finally get their Mona Lisa smiles embroidered realistically."

Rose Rushbrooke

ALDIE, VIRGINIA

May 2002

"May is lambing time in Virginia. Those crazy little creatures jumping all over the place with spring fever! Taking a class with Irene Kerr I learned stumpwork. In a book she recommends, RAISED EMBROIDERY, A PRACTICAL GUIDE TO DECORATIVE STUMPWORK, are instructions on how to create stumpwork sheep. This picture of happy lambs and their parents is my own design."

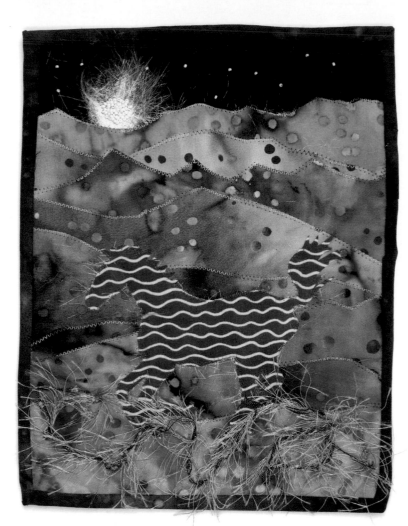

Crane Johnson
EAGLE, IDAHO

January 2006

"Sometimes you just have to create something that makes you smile. Don't you want to be the pony? I have been enamored of Angelina® fibers for the past year. An article in QUILTING ARTS MAGAZINE® led me to experiment with heating the fibers over a spool of thread. The resulting shape was just what I needed for the moon in my fantasy landscape."

Leigh Elking
SCOTTSDALE, ARIZONA

January 2006 (Opposite)

"Mer-horse"

"This Celtic 'Mer-horse' was inspired by a historical image of a primitive horse in a circular setting. I gave the horse Arabian-like features and a more realistic position. I expanded the knot work to complement the rectangular format. I used single- and double-layered chiffon on a commercial batik chosen for its water-like movement and color. Metallic thread and iridescent satin stitching give the images a glittery, underwater feeling."

Pam Wagner
PITTSBURGH, PENNSYLVANIA

February 2005

"Samurai Needles"

"Our horse, Samurai, was found in his stall with a mysterious oral injury a year ago. Twelve months, three vets, an equine hospital, and many thousands of dollars later, Sam had a misplaced veterinary hypodermic needle removed from his tongue! Using a horse-print fabric, I collaged the background, layered on a block of fabric with a burlap print, and raw-edge appliquéd the body of the hypodermic needle and the horse's head, cut from a commercial print. I scanned a photo of our horse into the computer and printed it onto PFD fabric, fusing the image to the quilt top. I then added red triangles to indicate pain around the horse's mouth, hand-painted details onto the hypodermic needle, and added foil embellishment."

Judith A. Imel

CARMICHAEL, CALIFORNIA • *February 2006*

"I was fascinated by the jellyfish exhibits at the Monterey Aquarium and inspired by a class with Ellen Anne Eddy. Sheer fabrics became jellyfish and added dimension to the water and seaweeds. I used my hand-dyed fabric for the background. Angelina® fibers added sparkle to the jellyfish's body. The fused binding was cut with a wavy edge, and I added a decorative stitch."

Beatrix von der Heiden

LEUN, GERMANY

January 2005

"And I was born centuries ago. And I will never die."

"Ondine's story is similar to THE LITTLE MERMAID by Hans Christian Andersen, but unlike the little mermaid, Ondine does not lose her life after she wrecks her relationship with Hans (who betrayed her). Instead, she goes on living forever...while he has to die. I manipulated a photo of myself by computer and printed it onto cotton fabric, adding a fish tail from silver tulle accented with silver fabric paint, machine quilting, and fabric beads. I printed Ondine's saying several times, placing it on top and bottom of the QuiltPage and between the waves."

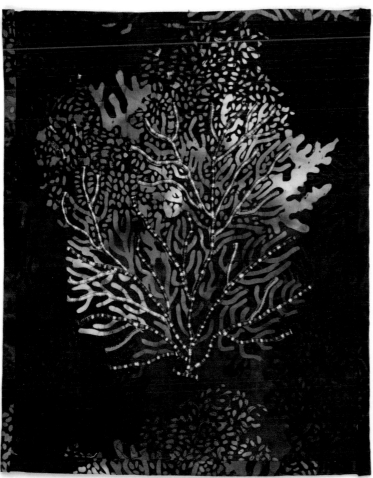

Carla C. Schardt

RESTON, VIRGINIA

March 2005

"A batik fabric with a multicolor print of sea corals is a favorite of mine. The question was how to use it. Why not make the design stand out and let the fabric speak for itself? By embellishing with a variegated polyester thread, both a sparkle and a texture were added. Now to try this with other fabric designs..."

Barbara A. Stewart

MIAMI, FLORIDA • *April 2002*

"My QuiltPages this year were made to match the month, each with a different technique. April seemed right for bunnies and pussy willows. I used CorelDRAW® to print the bunny on the fabric, threadpainted him, and attached him to a sky background. I added free-motion pussy willows, grass, and edging, using rayon thread throughout."

Creative Quilting: THE JOURNAL QUILT PROJECT

Landscapes & Special Places

Deep in every person's memory resides a special place— a homestead, a landscape, a vacation spot—a place of peace and tranquility, a place that speaks of happiness and loved ones. The QuiltPages in this chapter are all about those places. Capturing those special places and sharing them with others has long been the province of photographers, and before them, of landscape painters, particularly in the 18th and 19th centuries. Quilts provide an ideal medium for the exploration of how to convey these images, because the tangible quality of the quilts lends itself so well to the depiction of scenes and locations.

Many of the QuiltPages in this chapter deal with the tactile qualities of snow, frost, and ice; almost an equal number focus on the challenge of portraying the ocean, the beach, waves, sand, water, and lakes. Still others focus on landmarks and special experiences, such as seeing Christo's remarkable installation, "The Gates," in Central Park in New York City. Almost all of the quilts deal with the challenges of conveying light, whether it is sunlight, moonlight, or seasonal light, such as the light that creates soft colors in the blank whiteness of snow.

Here, the reader can take a quilt travelogue through places of the heart, real places, imaginary places, places shared, places of solitude, places of sorrow, and places of joy.

Creative Quilting: THE JOURNAL QUILT PROJECT

Alexandra Claire Tsubota

TORRANCE, CALIFORNIA

January 2006 (Opposite)

"January is always a bit of a letdown for me, just dealing with the holiday aftereffects of bills, excess weight, cleaning, and facing going back to work without another holiday until May. An invitation to a weekend trip to Sequoia started me thinking about snow, which led to this QuiltPage. I selected satin as my base fabric and divided it into four 'drifts' with satin stitching. I adapted a doodle from my sketchbook for the section above the 'drifts' and added a tree branch with Tsukineko® inks. For a long time I played with different quilting designs and auditioned various materials against the satin. Nothing was working. Finally, up against the deadline, I got lucky when some scraps of tulle arranged themselves fortuitously and gave me the idea of filling in one section with bits of tulle quilted with a swirl pattern. This is where showing up to work regardless of inspiration worked well for me! I do think that I was able to convey the things I love about snow, at least a little bit."

Deirdre Abbotts

WESTPORT, CONNECTICUT

February 2005 (Top right)

"Snowy Gates"

"I had the privilege of seeing Christo's 'The Gates' in New York's Central Park on opening day, as the saffron fabric was unfurled. A few days later I went again and got to Central Park early enough to see snow in all its glory! 'The Gates' were spectacular against the winter-clad trees, statues, and walkways. There were thousands of people enjoying the unusual closeness. It was wonderful! We ended up at the beautiful Angel Fountain at Bethesda Terrace, covered in a mantle of snow, with several birds perched on her. The photo I took from a distance shows the saffron gates all around her, creating a bright frame. The day was perfect! 'Snowy Gates' was a photograph printed on cotton using DURABrite® inks. Black thread outlines trees, limbs, and bushes. Adding additional branches where necessary, I then threadpainted with Polyneon thread in bright orange."

Karen Bettencourt

WOBURN, MASSACHUSETTS

February 2005 (Right)

"I'm Sick of Snow"

"I chose the Golden Rectangle as a unifying format for my QuiltPages because I liked the challenge of finding a solution for each month that fit within the form. In February, we had way too much snow where I live, and I took several digital photographs of the view, particularly around sunset. I liked the way the tree shadow lines rolled over the surface of the snow, so I emphasized that with machine quilting. I pieced the quilt after printing the rectangle on paper and then paper-pieced small squares of hand-dyed fabric."

Beth Billstrom

WACONIA, MINNESOTA

February 2006 (Left)

"Reflections II"

"Just when it seems the long Minnesota winter will never end, suddenly in my mind's eye, the colors of spring are reflected back wherever I look. Yes, April is coming! Here I used hand-painted fabrics, fused and soft-edged appliqué, Angelina® and Tintzl fibers, and then machine-quilted and machine-embroidered."

Joanna Price

SALEM, OREGON

June 2005 (Bottom left)

"I love to experiment with photo-transfer. This piece has a transferred photo of the Metolius River, one of the jewels of Central Oregon (and my favorite place on earth!). This cold, crystal-clear river bubbles up from deep volcanic springs to flow northward toward Mount Jefferson. Carefully chosen fabrics were stitched around the photo to expand the scene. Small bits of white fibers were attached to add depth to the rushing water and free-motion machine quilting finished the piece."

Sheri Hausman

HERMANN, MISSOURI

January 2006 (Opposite)

"Dawn from my front porch...how to capture the essence of January with bare, brittle outlines and just a glimmer of soft light? From a photograph I snapped while looking through the branches of my plum tree, the image is one of mystery ripe with new beginnings. The lighted window confirms this...anything can happen. I used a photo-transfer technique to copy the image, then burnished it to Habotai silk using automotive lacquer thinner. I then outlined the 'bones' of the image by machine with graduated silk and rayon threads. I carefully cut out the window and placed a tiny square of hand-dyed cotton behind the open space hoping to create light from within."

Linda Colsh

EVERBERG, BELGIUM • *January 2002*

"Freezing Fog"

"Farmers near my house go about the same monthly labors farmers here have done since the Middle Ages, even in 'Freezing Fog' when the winter world turns white. For my Journal Quilt, I wanted to do a series of calendar QuiltPages as my contemporary interpretation of the calendar pages in medieval illuminated manuscripts, many of which were created here in the Low Countries. THE BOOK OF HOURS and prayer books depicted the labors of each month, which rarely varied because people's lives were ruled by the available hours of daylight, the Church calendar, and farming cycles required to provide food. My January page shows a typical gray and silver Belgian winter day. Nearly invisible in the freezing fog is a farmer and his ewe. January in Belgium is mostly about getting through the winter, feeding the animals, and trying to stay warm. Fog is a difficult effect to capture in fabric; I used painted fusible web, layers of tulle, netting, and silvery threads over my own photo of the farmer and his sheep to achieve this effect. I used potato dextrin and thickened dyes to create the cracked ice patterns of the background fabric."

Linda K. Hayes
BATAVIA, ILLINOIS

January 2006

"Having bought a summer cabin on a small lake last fall, my husband and I have been spending most weekends there gutting the bathroom, tearing up floors, etc. We haven't had a chance yet to enjoy the beautiful setting. I only have winter pictures of it, and one of my favorites is of our backyard covered in snow. Our property ends after the row of snow-covered logs and on the other side is a wooded gully! I love gullies, so while this isn't our property, I pretend that it is. After transferring this photo to fabric, I machine-stitched some of the closer trees in the background, then added beads to accentuate the sunlight glistening on the snow. While I considered doing more stitching in the foreground, I decided to keep it sparse so the snow continued to look very soft."

Peggy Schroder
SWEET HOME, OREGON

August 2005

"The Santiam River"

"Last winter, I took this photograph of the view through our dining room window, showing our backyard. It is a much different view in summer with geese, ducks, fishing boats, and kayaks. My experience with threadpainting up to this point had only been with fiber-art postcards. I soon discovered that even a slightly larger piece takes oh, so much longer to do! The photo-transfer image was heat-set and then threadpainted heavily with metallic threads using free-motion sewing. I created an embroidery program to sew in the name of this QuiltPage."

Margaret Hunt
CLARKS HILL, SOUTH CAROLINA

January 2003 (Opposite)

"Mountains"

"January is a cold, chilly month, but it's always gorgeous in the mountains. The large fir tree was made entirely of thread on water-soluble stabilizer and stitched to the finished quilt with monofilament thread. Some hand-dyed fabric that had been aging around my sewing room was used for the sky and the background was layered fabric, to give the effect of foggy mountains. They were then threadpainted into submission to get the desired effect."

Lynne G. Harrill
GREENVILLE, SOUTH CAROLINA

June 2004 (Above)

"While visiting Charleston, South Carolina, in June 2004, I drove out to Folly Beach to take pictures, walk on the shore, and breathe the salt air. The photo that inspired this painting included some unattractive wooden boards and a dull gray sky. I manipulated the image to crop it and remove distracting elements such as the boards, added clouds, and greatly simplified the green sea oats. With this image as a guide, I painted white cotton with Setacolor fabric paint in a watercolor style and machine-quilted using a muslin batting."

July 2004 (Left)

"Late in July, I make an annual trip to my hometown in the mountains of western North Carolina. In this painted version of one of my photos, I used Paint Shop Pro® 7 to crop the image and change some elements in the photo. In this case, I eliminated a road and filled in with additional trees. I painted white cotton with Setacolor fabric paint in a watercolor style and machine-quilted using a muslin batting."

Kolla Bunch

LONDON, ENGLAND • *July 2004*

"The inspiration for this QuiltPage was a photo taken during a family vacation in Tenby, Wales. A tiny street in this seaside town was laden with details: windows, flowers, pillars, signs, a phone booth, etc. My challenge was to recreate that atmosphere in a quilt while simplifying it. To my surprise, this is my personal favorite of this year's Journal Quilts. The photograph provided the basic visual guideline during construction, and pieces were cut by hand and simply layered on until the desired effect was achieved, then fused, painted, and machine-quilted."

Maxine Farkas

LOWELL, MASSACHUSETTS • *January 2006*

"Lowell Henge"

"The 'bones' of mill buildings dot the landscape of the city where I live. Looking out my window I see granite remains in the most unlikely places . . . and who says I can't rebuild them in my mind's eye as something a little more mysterious? I used hand-dyed fabrics, fusible web, and thread to achieve this slightly disquieting effect."

Mary Beth Frezon

"Narrow View"

BRAINARD, NEW YORK • *August 2002*

"Lift up your eyes. Slice of life. During 2002, the image of the World Trade Center was always before me. In July, I made a small landscape quilt and set aside the trimmed edges. The little quilt was very peaceful and calm. I pieced the two bigger trimmings into this narrow window-like view. Even today, part of me sees the landscape beyond the window and part of me sees the tower-like shapes with the view seen through them."

Gloria Hansen

HIGHTSTOWN, NEW JERSEY • *April 2005*

"This image is based on a photo I took of an archway at Witley Court, Midlands, U.K., a once-grand house that is now an incredible ruin. It and the surrounding gardens are owned and cared for by English Heritage. The captivating contrast of textures led me to include a piece of metallic netting I bought at an English stitching show in my photo manipulation of the image onto silk. The archway's beautiful colors and textures were emphasized by machine stitching in different colors on the hand-painted cotton backing. I hope to create more work based on my photographs of this house."

Ruthie Powers

AUSTIN, TEXAS • *February 2006*

"I enjoyed making very small art quilts with single houses, so I decided that I would make a little village of houses for the February QuiltPage. I cut curved sides from fabric I had hand-painted for the body of the houses. Then I played around with each roof and the green foliage. I placed them on a background of painted cotton and cheesecloth and then added a small border. I used oil pastels to fill in bright colors and quilted with metallic threads. They are quite whimsical with their red and purple windows. This developed as a natural extension of the daily color collage design journals that I was doing after enjoying the demonstrations by Marlene Glickman at International Quilt Festival in Houston in 2005. Quilting with metallic thread added just the sparkle I wanted for my fantasy village. Recycled vintage rayon fabric and raw-edge appliqué found their way into the quilt, too."

Suzanne Mouton Riggio

WAUWATOSA, WISCONSIN • *May 2003*

"May Tornado Watch"

"When the sky turns dark with yellowish overtones, it is time to pay attention to the weather alerts. In my stash, I found tulle, lamé, and hand-dyed cottons in the exact shades needed to depict the foreboding, imminent nature of the approaching storm. Fusing, hand-beaded embellishment, machine embroidery, appliqué, and quilting complete the quilt."

Del Thomas

PLACENTIA, CALIFORNIA

August 2003 (Left)

"Passing Mars"

"On August 27, 2003, Mars passed near Earth, the closest it had come to our planet in nearly 60,000 years. The planets won't be in such close relationship for another 284 years. The mysterious red planet has always captured the imagination of scientists and science fiction writers. It stands out in the pantheon of stars and planets, glowing red against the night sky, and stirring urges for exploration. I conveyed this using fused hand-dyed and commercial cotton fabric, beads, and confetti pieces."

Sarah Ann Smith

CAMDEN, MAINE

January 2003 (Bottom left)

"Joshua's Window"

"My oldest son, then in second grade, was sometimes jealous of, yet fascinated by, my quilting. At the same time, I wanted to do a series on moons, and since I wanted my son to know he is an important part of my quilting, I asked his permission to base this first piece of the year on his artwork and poem, 'When I look out my window I see.' He was thrilled! I had never painted fabric, used metallic thread, or beaded a quilt before doing this, my first ever QuiltPage. I used a wash of blue transparent Setacolor to darken the sea on the side areas, and a wash of white mixed with a pearlescent blend to give the effect of moonlight on the water. I also fused sheer fabrics for the first time to make the stars and moon. I used a Pigma® pen to copy my son's handwriting around the edge of the piece, just like in his artwork, and finished the quilt with fused and machine-stitched appliqué and free-motion quilting."

Cathy Neri

MILFORD, PENNSYLVANIA

March 2002 (Opposite)

"During our first trip to the Florida Keys, my husband Mark and I used my new digital camera to take sunset photos from a different vantage point every evening. Afterwards I used Bubble Jet Set® to transfer this digital image of a Key West sunset to cotton fabric. The image was then threadpainted with variegated rayon, metallic, and hologram Madeira® threads."

Creative Quilting: THE JOURNAL QUILT PROJECT

Linda S. Schmidt
DUBLIN, CALIFORNIA

February 2004 (Opposite)

"While trying to develop an online 'Elements in Fabric' class for www.QuiltUniversity.com, I experimented with different techniques to create the illusion of water streaming over rock and capture the iridescent light it gives off. Oddly enough, the first thing most people comment on is how cool the 'cheater' forest fabric is, not on all the work I put into the water effect. Go figure. I painted the sky with Setacolor, fused on the 'cheater' fabric trees with Steam-a-Seam II Lite®, then created the grassy hills and rocks with puff paint. The water was created in the distance by laying a series of iridescent fabrics over water fabric. As the stream comes into the foreground, I used iridescent melted cracked ice over water fabric. After layering the whole scene, I sewed it to Totally Stable™ with invisible thread and a tiny zigzag stitch, and then ripped the stabilizer off."

Ann B. Graf
HOUSTON, TEXAS

March 2005 (Right)

"Am I crazy? Looking back, I can't believe I cut out all those individual daisies—it took days! When I found the stamp for the tree, the whole idea came together—hills and trees in the background and a field of daisies in the foreground. The trees were created by using a two-piece stamp; one part was for the trunk, and the other for the leaves. It required a steady hand to line up the leaves with the trunks. I started with a daisy template and enlarged and reduced to get various sizes that were traced onto fusible web with a paper backing, individually cut out by hand, and arranged on the quilt before fusing."

Judith A. Imel
CARMICHAEL, CALIFORNIA

March 2005 (Bottom right)

"This Journal QuiltPage represents memories of a visit to our daughter's 15 wooded acres in Idaho. Using my hand-dyed and commercial fabrics, I cut trees freehand, fused them, and then added more details with thread. I used Angelina® fibers to make the flames of the fire sparkle. Raw-edge appliqué and machine-embroidery techniques were also used."

Sally K. Field
HAMPDEN, MAINE

March 2004 (Left)

"When we were on the Outer Banks of North Carolina in March, I took a digital photograph of the Hatteras Light. Because of dune erosion, the lighthouse had been moved further inland since we saw it the year before. For my first representational piece, I enlarged my photo on the computer and traced it for pattern pieces. The appliqué fabric was fused onto Pellon® interfacing and machine-appliquéd."

Betsy True
ALEXANDRIA, VIRGINIA

February 2006 (Bottom left)

"I enjoy interpreting photos in fabric. I am planning a large quilt of a wave crashing against a rocky shore and used this QuiltPage to try out techniques. I took the picture in La Jolla, California, and used commercial fabrics, fusing, hand beading, and machine quilting in this piece. To depict foam thrown off by the wave, I hand-stitched clear beads and fused tiny white squares using a snip technique taught by Lynda Poole Prioleau. I also experimented by fusing the binding."

Susan Brittingham
FLOYD COUNTY, VIRGINIA

January 2006 (Opposite)

"A spring-like day in January inspired an outing to a nearby city to walk back in time, visit my old college campus, and stroll through neighborhoods filled with old Victorian houses. I have always loved Victorian domestic architecture, especially the 'sorting hats' that top their fanciful turrets. This quilt was constructed using a machine-appliqué method that I developed and call 'Upside-down Appliqué,' because the initial sewing is done from the wrong side, or upside-down. The basis for this quilt was a photo manipulated to create a mirror-image line drawing that I printed onto tear-away stabilizer. The next step was to attach the stabilizer to a background fabric, then appliqué each element of the design from the wrong side, using the stabilizer drawing as a stitching guide."

Susan Madden

AUSTIN, TEXAS • *February 2005*

"The Gates"

"'The Gates' was a magical transformation of Central Park by Christo. I used just two different photographs to convey the feeling of a seemingly endless procession of 'Gates.' Adobe® Photoshop® was used to print the multiple images on the top row; the bottom photo varied in size and image cropping. Photos were printed on inkjet iron-on transfer paper, ironed onto cotton broadcloth, and machine-stitched onto the pieced background. I tried to incorporate my small square of orange, or saffron, 'Gate fabric' but it just seemed to lose its vibrancy and magic once I anchored it down, so I left it off."

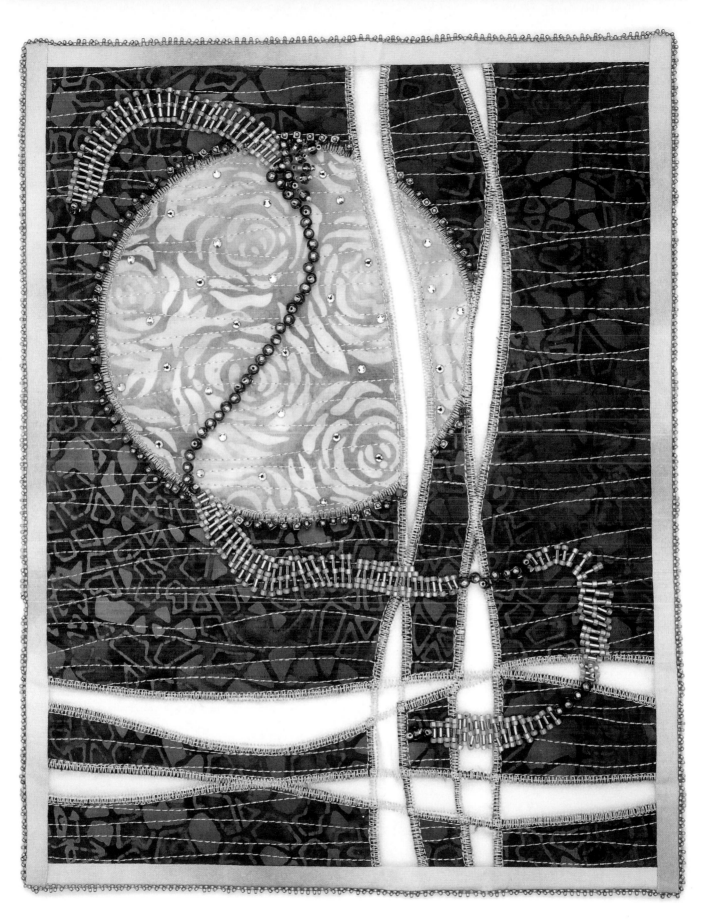

Jo Grooms

CHELAN FALLS, WASHINGTON • *August 2003*

"I had been tossing ideas around in my head about how to create sheer segments in my quilts. I decided reverse machine appliqué was the best method, and this is my first attempt at it, using silk organza, hand beading, and machine quilting. The sheer appliqué was accomplished by layering: the top piece, the sheer, the batting, and then the backing. After machine-stitching my design, I cut away the top layer, then turned it over and cut away the backing and the batting, being careful not to cut into the sheer fabric beneath."

Creative Quilting: THE JOURNAL QUILT PROJECT

Nancy G. Cook
CHARLOTTE, NORTH CAROLINA

February 2006 (Opposite)

"On a cold, sunny, spring day, I sketched the arching branches of forsythia. Thank goodness for signs of spring! After a long winter, spring is welcome. Life returns. Using the sketch, I located a wonderful piece of fabric by Heide Stoll Weber with colors to evoke the atmosphere of spring. I really enjoyed playing with the many colors of green and yellow. I used free-motion quilting to draw the design, with straight stitching for the forsythia branches and a pattern stitch for the flowers. Free-motion stitching created grasses, bushes, trees, and water. Several different yellows give a sense of depth to the forsythia bush. My Journal Quilt this year is based on surface design techniques."

Kathy Angel Lee
OLD ORCHARD BEACH, MAINE

March 2005 (Top right)

"A critique by a local artist made me think about the importance of the light source. For example, what time of day is it? Where is the light coming from? Is it from your mind? Therefore, I tried to work on the light source in my Journal Quilt series on landscapes. To complete this spring scene, I tried Angelina® fibers, shaded green threads, a variety of green fabrics to capture the airy feeling of spring leaves (for the bushes and new growth), and free-motion stitching. I layered the background in different fabrics to give a sense of rolling hills. Hand-painted, hand-dyed cotton fabric was used."

Christine L. Adams
ROCKVILLE, MARYLAND

September 2005 (Right)

"Dance in the light of the pale cold moon to the sound of a wild violin"—Erika Fawcett

"Year 2005 was going to be a difficult one—I was working full time and also immersed in writing my master's thesis. Fortunately, I didn't know just how hard the semester would be. A 'heart episode' in April hospitalized me for a week. My personal theme, 'Simple Pleasures Times Nine,' became more significant and included the wonder of a moonlit night, my Journal QuiltPage. I used raw-edged appliqué, free-motion quilting, fused binding, buttons, and metallic thread embellishment."

Creative Quilting: THE JOURNAL QUILT PROJECT

Frances Holliday Alford
AUSTIN, TEXAS

June 2003 (Opposite)

"I have always enjoyed the unusual architecture of buildings made to depict other items. The Orange House reminds me of the 'tourist courts' of the mid-century made to honor regional attractions. I think it would be fun to live in a house shaped like an orange, with a lemon for a chimney and a grapefruit garage. I hand-painted fabric and used free-motion quilting."

Carol Ann Perkins
BROOKFIELD, ILLINOIS

January 2005 (Top right)

"My 2005 January QuiltPage is my first public offering. I challenged myself to use my hand-painted fabric and to try raw-edge appliqué and threadpainting on the tree and leaves, my first time using these techniques. The tree symbolizes my having withstood the storms of life and standing in the sunrise of a new day. I also used metallic thread embellishment on this piece."

Sandra Betts
SAINT JOHN, NEW BRUNSWICK, CANADA

July 2005 (Right)

"I have always lived next to the ocean, and the vagaries of its moods have always been an influence on my life. It inspires, excites, calms, soothes. I love to sit and watch it at all times of day and night. The intricacy of the sea spray inspires me time and again to try to capture its fleeting patterns. This QuiltPage portrays the incoming waves and approaching overcast skies. Hand-dyed and -painted fabric formed the seascape and the exposed and submerged rocks. Free-motion metallic threadpainting defined the water and rocks. Angelina® fibers were added and enhanced with cellophane that had been painted and then heat-distressed and cut into the shapes I needed to define the spray and foam."

Deanna Smith Apfel
PHILO, CALIFORNIA

May 2005 (Left)

"I think of Moloka'i, Hawaii, as Philo West, a small island with no stoplights, a small population, and a gorgeous natural setting. We have redwoods, they have palm trees...and mangoes...and papayas...and trade winds like silk on your skin. Beach time, exploration, and palm tree planting sum up this relaxing vacation. I have been using dupioni silk in my work because I love the luminosity. It perfectly captured the color of the sea and a glorious Hawaiian sunset and reminded me of those silky breezes."

Amy Eileen Koester
PALM COAST, FLORIDA

June 2003 (Bottom left)

"Fish Taco"

"'Fish Taco' commemorates a special camping trip to San Felipe, memorable to me because of many firsts: it was the first time I had been in Baja, the first time I had ever heard of a fish taco, and it was my first real adventure on my own following my divorce. I smile every time I look at this QuiltPage and can feel the sun on my face and almost taste the salt from the Sea of Cortez. I created my fish taco by making a separate tortilla quilt and folding it in half. I fused the fish to black batting, stitched the outline of each fish, cut them out, and glued them inside the taco shell. The black batting gives more depth to the stack of fish. The cabbage is paper that I ran through an office shredder, then a paper crimper, and then glued it inside the taco shell. Commercial fabric, strip-pieced background, hand- and machine-appliqué, and machine quilting were all used."

Lisa Konkel
FAIR LAWN, NEW JERSEY

February 2006 (Opposite)

"We are in the middle of getting our house ready for a move. It feels as though it is bursting at the seams with all the clutter that needs to be sorted, packed, or removed. I guess this year I'll learn how to pare down to the basic essentials (like fabric, paint, and beads) and find out how much of my quilting stuff I really don't use. For this QuiltPage, commercial fabrics and raw-edge appliqué were the techniques employed."

Sat Sansar Khalsa Best

FLAGSTAFF, ARIZONA • *July 2005*

"The act of transformation, of becoming, seeking the light, is central to my feeling about my own growth. All creatures go toward the light. Moths and moonlight...yin. This tropical moth was painted and threadpainted, cut out, and sewn on the quilt, according to Ellen Anne Eddy's technique, and the background was bleached with dishwasher soap. The trees are made of heated and painted Tyvek® and the cloud and lower quilt were shaded with chiffon and painted WonderUnder®, both according to Maggie Grey's techniques."

Marcia Ann Kuehl

CAPISTRANO BEACH, CALIFORNIA

February 2006

"Winter in Hawaii"

"My 2006 Journal Quilt series is based on trees. The single tree has always been dear to my heart. In Wisconsin, the countryside is marked with fields that have a single tree standing among the neatly plowed fields. Each tree has its own strength of character as it stands the ultimate test of time against nature. Seasons come and go yet the tree stands in all its glory. Here, the single tree is a palm tree on a Hawaiian beach. Procion Dyes® created the greens and blues of Hawaii, capturing the warmth of a tropical climate. The empty beach indicates winter, while the machine-pieced binding reflects the continual beach line. The linear stop-and-start quilting technique, with low-contrast color thread, follows the background contours, creating the feeling of depth and movement. I used raw-edge appliqué as well as machine piecing and linear quilting. This year's Journal Quilts also represent my first attempt to work in the small format of the project, and my first observation was that despite the small size, every aspect took as long, or longer, than a larger quilt."

Julie Wolkoff

WELLESLEY, MASSACHUSETTS

January 2006

"My January QuiltPage reflects New Year's Eve in St. Martin. As I watched the fireworks over the water, I wondered if I could translate them into a quilt. I asked myself, 'How does the light reflect on the water?' 'How would I create sparkle?' My favorite part turned out to be the palm tree. My first was solid black and very subtle. I tried again, and the mottled print was too light. Finally, I put the mottled print tree over the solid one, decided it worked, and ironed it down before I could change my mind or obsess over it. In creating the fireworks, I modified the techniques taught by Helen Marshall in her QuiltUniversity class. An irregularly shaped appliqué patch under the fireworks creates the base color, and the fireworks are a mixture of variegated cotton and rayon threads. With the feed dogs of my sewing machine up, I pulled the fabric back and forth to create the jagged points. The final touch was the addition of copper and white glitter on top of the thread."

Carol J. Moore

TORONTO, ONTARIO, CANADA • *February 2006*

"Canadians Dream of the Caribbean in February!"

"I'd been experimenting with making fiber-art postcards by layering strands of hand-dyed raw wool fleece onto black felt, pinning water-soluble stabilizer over the top, quilting, and then dissolving the stabilizer to see what emerged. For this piece, I attempted a larger format and wanted to distinguish the color fields with distinctly different directions in the quilting. When done, I was surprised to see that it reminded me of the lush Caribbean jungle as it meets that unbelievably warm blue sea, a lovely vision on a cold, snowy night. Hand-dyed raw wool fleece, commercial felt, free-motion quilting with hand-dyed cotton thread, and cotton batik were all used."

needed to live in those early times. Later, with more advanced media to work with, artists painted their human subjects with oils and sculpted them in marble. Whether it was an early religious painting of a saint, the image carefully conveying accurate anatomical details of muscle and bone, or an Impressionist's gentle, romantic view of people enjoying a Sunday afternoon with friends on a French riverside—the same challenge of how to capture the human form prevailed.

The QuiltPages in this chapter are often depictions of real people, either the artist herself or people whom she knows or loves. In other examples, you see self-portraits—often conveyed with photo-transfer—revealing harsh emotion or, conversely, with abstract humor, wit, or whimsy. It is interesting to note that the highly individualistic and sometimes fanciful self-portraits created in fabric and thread often say more about the person than the most accurate painting could ever reveal. Other QuiltPages feature faces and figures taken from ancient history and mythology, and one highly original piece creates a "Face of Faces"—a composite image made up of parts of the photos of 36 schoolchildren.

Maria Elkins

DAYTON, OHIO • *May 2003*

"Sarah"

"On this portrait I tried to paint quickly without being too much of a perfectionist. My personal challenge is to try to work more spontaneously and to develop a freer style. I used erasable watercolors, fabric paint, and metallic threads."

Maria Elkins

DAYTON, OHIO • *May 2003*

September 2005

"This 'Maria' is the first print from my Beginning Lithography class at Wright State University. I rarely do self-portraits, but for my first lithograph I wanted something that would be easy to draw so I could concentrate on the process and not the subject. I used a stone lithograph and Superior Threads Rainbows™."

Creative Quilting: THE JOURNAL QUILT PROJECT

Pamela Allen

KINGSTON, ONTARIO, CANADA

May 2003 (Opposite)

"Having decided on portraits for [my theme] this year, I thought I would tackle a double portrait in honor of my wedding anniversary this month. Picasso often depicted the same face front-on and in profile. Using the same strategy, I tried to capture both my husband and me. I also tried to get a texture and liveliness into it using big-stitch embroidery rather than machine quilting and enhanced the raw-edge appliqué and embroidery with eyes created with Bubble Jet Set®. I like how the two are joined by a kiss!"

July 2005 (Right)

"After a decade of cutting my own hair, a friend convinced me to go to a real hairdresser. Ack! Talk about a bad hair day! And it cost me $55 to boot! Stringing multicolored buttons on wire made it even easier to depict how bad my hair was!"

Sherry Boram

PENDLETON, INDIANA

July 2005

"Copper Man"

"A centuries-old copper ornament from Spiro Mound, Oklahoma, meets 21st-century art materials! When I used copper mesh on malachite green fabric, 'Copper Man' became an exercise in texture. The design was inspired by nature where copper and malachite often appear together."

6: Faces & Figures

Sandra Townsend Donabed NEWTON, MASSACHUSETTS • *January 2006*

"The Golfer"

"I am marooned in Florida because of my husband's love of golf. I do like it here for the pleasant weather and beautiful flowers, but I find that I cannot do any work in this atmosphere. I go home to Boston for a week of quiet studio time. I try to meet deadlines and fail; I try to work and other things come up—it's very frustrating. In 1981 I developed 'floor quilts,' which were simply small exercises that I restricted by using only those little pieces that had fallen to the floor around my worktable. These snippets were arranged and held down with pieces of nylon netting so I could avoid actual appliqué. The idea was to be completely spontaneous and not obsess about technique. I return to this continually for fun and inspiration."

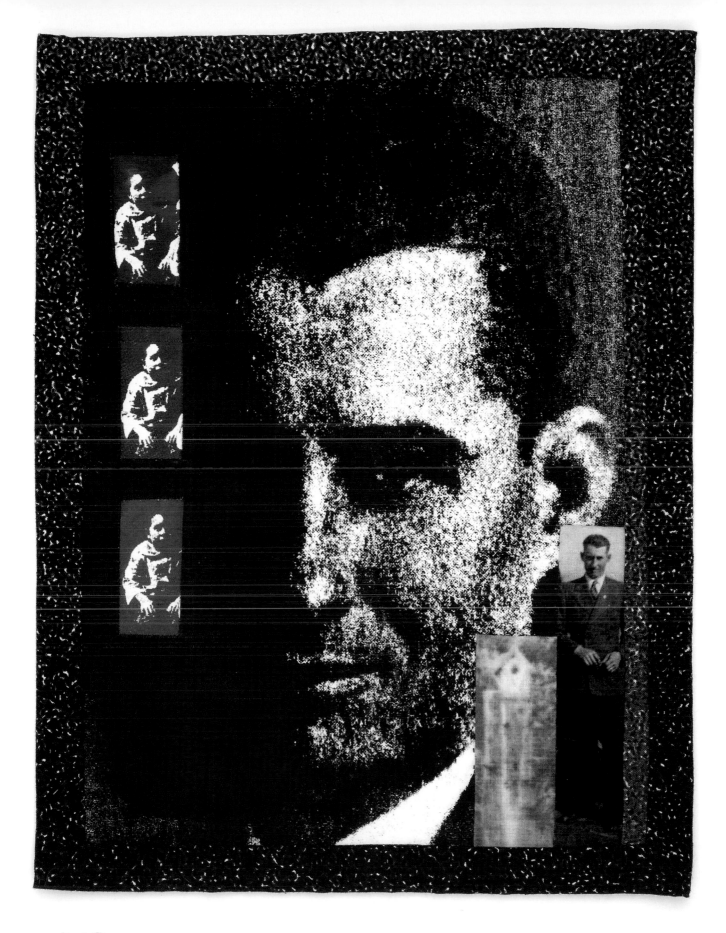

Pat Owoc

ST. LOUIS, MISSOURI • *January 2003*

"Oscar Cook, my father, was a kind and gentle man who loved his family and the land that he had farmed for 40 years. Dad slowly disappeared, becoming confused and weak as Alzheimer's progressed. His last woodworking projects, his birdhouses, also disappear with time. I used silkscreen, spirit transfer, and cyanotype to create this QuiltPage. Postscript: My father died May 18, 2005, of pneumonia and the effects of Alzheimer's."

6: Faces & Figures

Betty Cabell Ford

SILVER SPRING, MARYLAND

January 2004 (Left)

"Babe in the Woods"

"A self-portrait often expresses feelings of doubt about one's creative and artistic ability. With each new piece, the artist must once again face fear of failure and stand before the work like an uninitiated child. I painted the sky fabric with Setacolor, scanned one of my baby photos, printed it on broadcloth, and appliquéd it to the snow fabric. I chose not to fuse the trees to achieve more roundness. Finally, I painted on the finished quilt to give the trees a wintry feel and more definition."

Dori Tighe

MILFORD, PENNSYLVANIA

February 2006 (Bottom left)

"As my mother slips ever deeper into Alzheimer's, my QuiltPages reflect her life. Some celebrate her life; this one interprets her unraveling and my attempts to halt it with the increasing list of drugs prescribed by her physicians. I used inkjet printing on fabric with Bubble Jet Set® as well as slicing, unraveling, and weaving fabric strips."

Del Thomas

PLACENTIA, CALIFORNIA

July 2002 (Opposite)

"Missing Constance"

"Two years after my English friend Constance Howard died, I can now think of her without tears and overwhelming grief. For this homage to her, I used my computer to print a photo of her on batik fabric and then modified it with fused fabric, fabric markers, and colored pencils. Fused trees and foliage were free-motion quilted."

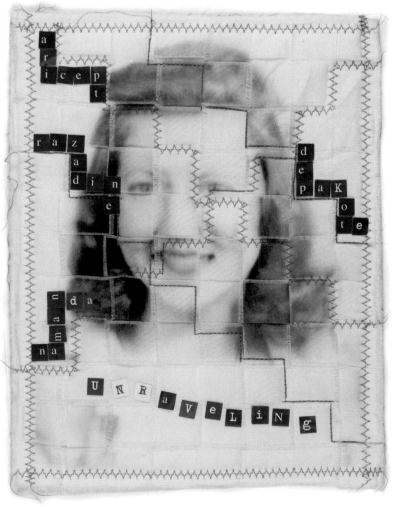

del 2002

6: Faces & Figures

Creative Quilting: THE JOURNAL QUILT PROJECT

Jamie Fingal
ORANGE, CALIFORNIA

January 2003 (Opposite)

"Woman/Changes"

"I decided that I wanted to use a woman's face in each quilt to represent myself...an artist, mother, wife, daughter, sister, Girl Scout volunteer, etc. My art quilt, 'Beauty of a Woman,' was shown at Road to California and was my first entry into a quilt show. Then I entered it into the Sacred Threads show in the spiritual category. My friendship group, the Cut-Loose Quilters, began its second year. My stepson Jim celebrated his 20th birthday, saying goodbye to those teenage years. I really enjoyed layering the fabrics, the use of contrast, and another opportunity to practice free-motion machine quilting. I used rubber stamping with acrylic paint, along with batik and hand-dyed fabrics. I wrote the text by hand, then machine-quilted each letter."

Sandra Ealy
WASHINGTON, D.C.

January 2006 (Top right)

"Hi, I Am A..."

"I am many people. I am a wife, mother, and grand-mother. I am a daughter, sister, and aunt. I am an African-American Queen. I am a woman going through menopause. I am a dreamer. I am a lover of life. I am, most of all, a quilter."

February 2006 (Right)

"Healing Hand"

"I know what you are saying: 'Not another hand!' The Eye of Horus, an Egyptian symbol, is said to have healing powers. This hand and symbol called to me, since I was calling to be healed. My hands are bothering me, and the doctor gave me an injection in my right hand. I don't want to continue getting injections for the pain. So, I am channeling the power of the eye within me."

Kate Kline

TULSA, OKLAHOMA • *February 2006*

"It all started with a piece of my hand-painted fabric that was bold and gritty-looking and just called out for an image of youthful energy. Some images of my son Jeremy when he was a teenager were perfect for the background, and I added graffiti to fill it out. Then I realized that the entire piece was a subconscious desire to celebrate Jeremy. Nine years ago in February he was diagnosed with the cancer that was to take his life at age 27. It is a milestone for me that my art can now celebrate his life, rather than mourn his death. The background fabric was created using a monoprint technique learned in a workshop with Charlotte Yde. Fabric paints were applied to an acetate sheet over a masking-tape resist. The acetate was then flipped over onto the plain white fabric and pressed with my hands to facilitate movement of the paint, then removed. When the paint dried it was heat-pressed with an iron. The central image was scanned into my computer and manipulated in Photoshop®. Using a photo-transfer method also learned from Charlotte, the graffiti images and the central image were printed with an inkjet printer onto matte photo paper. They were then coated with gel medium and ironed onto fabric. The images were cut out and fused to the background."

Kevan Rupp Lunney   EAST BRUNSWICK, NEW JERSEY • *March 2003*

"The Stress Quilt or Compass Askew"

"Mom appears in my lens, modeling on black-and-white TV. Responsibilities crowd my head. I dangle from my ear. This is a self-portrait, enlarged to an 8" x 10" print; the local copy shop changed the image to a color negative and copied it onto heat-transfer paper. The black part at the bottom was white on the original photo."

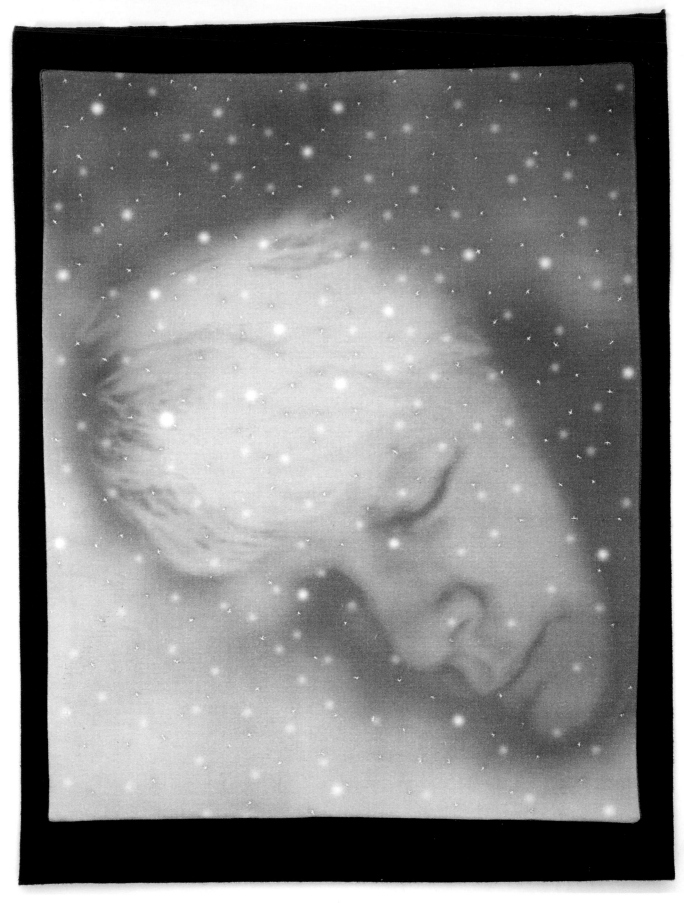

Terry Grant

PORTLAND, OREGON • *March 2002*

"I was traveling back and forth between Oregon and Colorado in 2002. The change in altitude was dramatic. In Colorado, I just wanted to sleep. I would dream of the snow falling and drifting all around me, my white hair becoming drifting snow. I carefully laid my face directly on the scanner plate and scanned. In Photoshop® I used the airbrush tool to add in the blue and white background areas. I created the snow on a second layer, blurred to soften the snowflakes, and printed it on fabric treated with Bubble Jet Set®."

Sandra Betts

SAINT JOHN, NEW BRUNSWICK, CANADA

July 2002

"Memories Are Made Of This"

"Hot, sunny summer days are spent at the beach with my grandchildren playing in the water, exploring the tidal pools, running races, building dams and other grand engineering feats, watching the soaring gulls, the harbor seals, and the fishing cormorants. We play from sunup to sundown. The saltwater smell, the sounds of the children's laughter, the heat of the sun, the feel of the sand, the cool, refreshing sea breeze, the smell of fresh raspberries, and the sounds of the sea will always evoke the wonderful euphoria of summers with the children and their amazing curiosity that is so easily satisfied with a simple answer and demonstration. To create the silhouettes, I scanned pictures of my grandchildren, then cropped and reworked them to give me their outlines. I then cut these outlines from black fabric and fused them to fabric that I painted to give the impression of the children's joy and boisterous play after a long day."

June 2005

"Oh, The Joy Of Turning Back Time!"

"In June I attended my 45th graduation reunion. At that time we revisited many of the places we had frequented in our youth. Wanting to recapture the carefree feelings of that time, I was inspired to depict one of our most vivid memories, but from today's perspective. Hand-dyed and commercial fabrics were cut freeform and fused to a background to create the landscape. These were then threadpainted with variegated and metallic threads. I sketched the figures and then cut them from hand-dyed fabric. When they were fused and stitched, I used watercolor paints to shade and shape the figures."

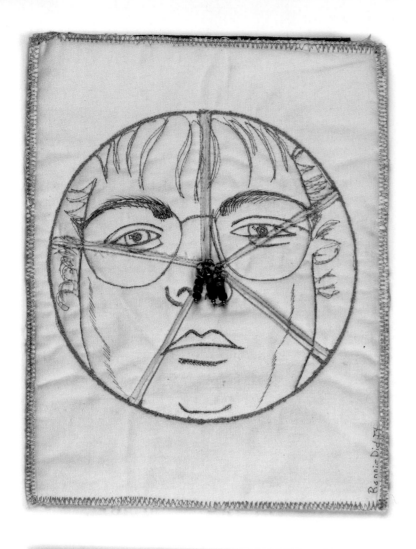

Rhonda (Ronnie) Doyal

CENTERVILLE, OHIO

September 2002 (Left)

"Breaking Out, Finding the Artist Within"

"Ah, the last QuiltPage for the year. Since this one will have no partner, it is two quilts in one. They are self-portraits, in my quest to find my artistic voice. The top quilt is plain, but if you open it up to reveal the quilt underneath, you will see a colorful me trying to get out. It is hand-painted, and the faces are free-motion quilted. I took a picture of myself and, using Photoshop®, converted it into a line image that I then transferred to two pieces of white fabric using Pigma® pens. I made each of these into individual quilts. I painted one and outlined the face, then left it un-quilted. The other, I left plain and free-motion machine-quilted the lines. Then I cut the center into wedges and sewed beads onto a couple of wedge tips. I placed the plain quilt on top of the painted one and sewed around all four edges. Now a single quilt with double layers, the cut wedges of the plain top provide a window to the colorful quilt underneath."

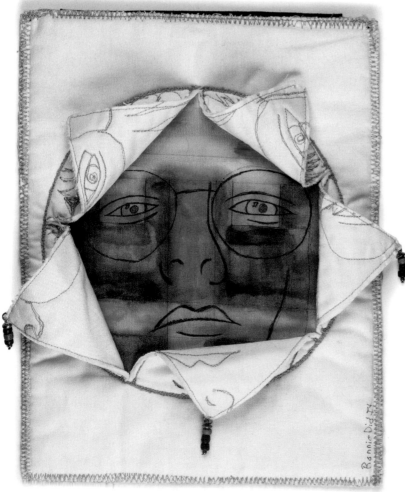

Rhonda (Ronnie) Doyal

CENTERVILLE, OHIO

February 2003 (Right)

"This was a year of self-examination for me. This quilt depicts my body as I see it. It is not, nor will it ever look like, the body of a 20-year-old. It is, however, the body of a wife and mother, and I would not trade those roles for anything. I am happy with myself, but it took me my whole life to get to that place in my mind. I call this appliqué technique 'On the Road Appliqué.' Instead of turning the edges under, as in traditional appliqué, I rolled the edges up. It makes for a soft, raggedy edge, which I thought suited this application perfectly."

September 2003 (Bottom right)

"All of Me"

"Each quilt during this year of self-examination was an expression of a piece of my self. This last one is my whole self. The conclusion: I like myself. The hair on this was done one strand of thread at a time. I used several shades of red and orange, with metallic copper and gold thrown in for good measure. Each strand is knotted on top of the fabric. When all the hair was finished, I used a piece of fusible interfacing on the back side of the fabric to insure that the threads would not come out."

Sidney Davis Jostes
NAPERVILLE, ILLINOIS

June 2003

"Mysterious One"

"This QuiltPage grew from photos of my daughter taken in natural light. Ashley has beautiful, mysterious eyes that suggest something universal and poetic. The background pattern in the quilt was invented from strands of her hair as they fold beneath her head. A colored pencil class I took inspired me to paint with Prismacolor® pencils on cotton. I staged a photo shoot of my daughter on my deck in natural afternoon light. The most unusual photo was cropped and enlarged at my local copy store. I traced the photocopy onto PFD white cotton with a washable pen. The cotton drawing was ironed to freezer paper for stability and colored in with layer upon layer of Prismacolor® pencils, until the white cloth was totally covered. The top layers of colored pencil burnished the lower layers, creating a smooth surface and obscuring the weave of the fabric. Some areas of the face and hair were enhanced with iridescent paint. The final portrait was sealed with a polymer gloss medium. The top was quilted first with invisible thread, then sewn to the back fabric on two sides and turned inside-out. The raw edges at the top and bottom were stitched with peacock Glitter™ thread."

April 2004

"Image"

"My youngest teenage daughter was suffering from self-doubt, even though she's slim, beautiful, and wonderfully creative. Her skin is lovely, and her hair is beautiful. She doesn't realize it, but she is as nearly perfect as it's possible to be. This QuiltPage is a comment on the way our culture encourages teenage girls to feel great dissatisfaction with their bodies and themselves. I chose the composition for my piece from a black-and-white photograph I took of a store window display. The background fabric was created by accordion folding a piece of black fabric and discharging it with thickened bleach. The large foreground figure on the left was cut from a piece of fabric I created using thickened Procion® MX dye, stamped and painted on white fabric, with an additional layer of red-dyed silk organza. The text was typed on top of the figure, and the result was printed onto fabric treated with Bubble Jet Set®. I fused the girl onto the discharged background, and appliquéd a piece of tulle-like fabric, cut from a piece of lace, over a portion of the girl's body. Each letter of the text was fused down separately and enhanced with textile paint."

Sheri Hausman

"Les Amants"

HERMANN, MISSOURI • *February 2005*

Photograph in quilt © Timothy Shonnard

"I love this picture! I call this couple 'Les Amants', 'The Lovers', and am envious of their comfortable sharing. I recently became engaged to my high school sweetheart. Two years ago, after 35 years, he walked back into my life...when he proposed, I accepted. This journal page was my Valentine's Day gift to him last year. The faces of the older couple on top of the wedding dress brocade represent the bond that comes from loving someone day in, day out...something I look forward to."

Frances Caple
ISLE OF LEWIS, SCOTLAND

January 2006 (Opposite)

"I wanted to explore the idea of producing a whole-cloth quilt by creating an image in Photoshop® and then printing it onto the whole journal page. First, I painted a background fabric. I created my design in Photoshop® Elements by overlaying three separate layers over my background, then flattening all the layers to print it onto fabric. The piece was then machine-quilted, bound with monoprinted Lutradur®, and beaded with handmade fabric and paper beads. For the beads, I used elongated triangles of fabric or paper, which is a great way to use leftovers. I used a silver pen along some edges. With the wrong side up, I put a little glue along the edges, then, starting with one straight edge, I rolled them up to create the beads."

Lyn Wolf Jackson
BILLINGS, MONTANA

February 2002 (Top right)

"Off Balance on a Slippery Slope"

"Last month I began to think of leaving a long career. Is my life carved in stone? Did it matter? February was a month of unexpected happenings, some good, some not. I landed on my feet."

June 2002 (Right)

"Pod Person"

"And the day came when the risk it took to remain tight inside the bud was more painful than the risk it took to blossom."
— Anais Nin

"I cannot say it better. I left the career this month. A new life awaits."

Penny Mateer
PITTSBURGH, PENNSYLVANIA

March 2005 (Left)

"Cat and Fiddle"

"One of my favorite artists is Jacob Lawrence. Inspired by his work, this quilt is my first attempt at creating my own figurative style. I drew from the rich tradition of jazz and from my own experience to create this QuiltPage. By working small, I hope to continue to develop my style and to expand to larger pieces."

June 2004 (Bottom left)

"I have learned in this project to experiment, and the key is to work small. I began by stitching ribbons to a background. As I worked I discovered a marsh in Nantucket. Trying a new technique, I created the water by bobbin drawing. When I finished I thought of my mother-in-law who loves Nantucket and now lives with Alzheimer's disease."

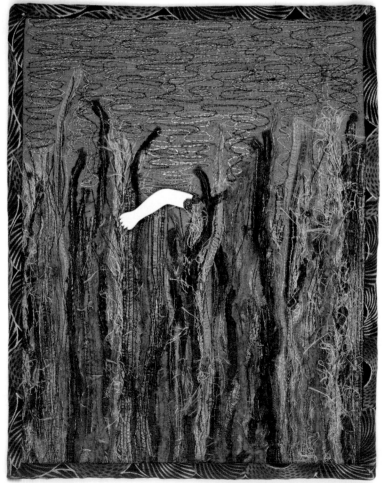

Karylee Doubiago
ADAMS, MASSACHUSETTS

May 2005 (Opposite)

"I woke up tired today. I stayed that way the entire month. Life is wearing me thin. I don't have that glimmer in my eyes, that strength in my soul. Some days the depression is so hard to take; sometimes the sheer mental fatigue is too much to bear. No matter how many hours I sleep at night, the mornings bring the same thing: I woke up tired today. I used black-and-white photographs cropped and printed onto fabric, along with dyes and fabric paints."

CHAPTER 6: FACES & FIGURES

Kathie Briggs
CHARLEVOIX, MICHIGAN

April 2004 (Left)

"The calendar may claim spring is here, but in April, winter persists in northern Michigan. Another cold, dreary day prolongs my 'April Blahs,' a close cousin of Holly Golightly's 'Mean Reds' (think Audrey Hepburn in BREAKFAST AT TIFFANY'S) but with a decidedly brown hue. I drew the facial features with a fine tip (.005) brown Pigma® pen and then colored with pencils. The face was framed with thread and fibers trapped under tulle scraps, then layered between sheer ribbons and fabric with free-motion machine stitching."

Lutgard Gerber-Billiau
GRIMBERGEN, BELGIUM

July 2005 (Bottom left)

"This will be a big year since, in October, I will be 50. Here I printed my face on fabric, in all different sizes. Beginning with the first QuiltPage, I tried to reuse at least one fabric in the following page to achieve a kind of continuity. The flower and the eyes are also repeated in almost every 2005 QuiltPage. So—me again—surrounded by beads, a flower, an eye...just me!"

Margaret Hunt
CLARKS HILL, SOUTH CAROLINA

January 2006 (Opposite)

"Forest Elf"

"I have been taking a great workshop at Jan Girod's Fiber on a Whim in Atlanta. Every month we do a new technique, and by the end of the year we will have a book showing all these great fiber art techniques. I decided last fall I was going to do a different lady for each month this year. But after taking Jan's class, I decided to incorporate at least one of the techniques we learned into my lady of the month, so I painted the Tyvek® with Lumiere® and had great fun turning it into all those realistic-looking, shiny leaves that form her hair. I free-motion quilted the leaves and drew the lady's face with Pigma® pens, Prismacolor® pencils, and gel pens. I then embellished her a little with torn strips of lamé and some great gold junk fabric I had. Voila, elle est complete!"

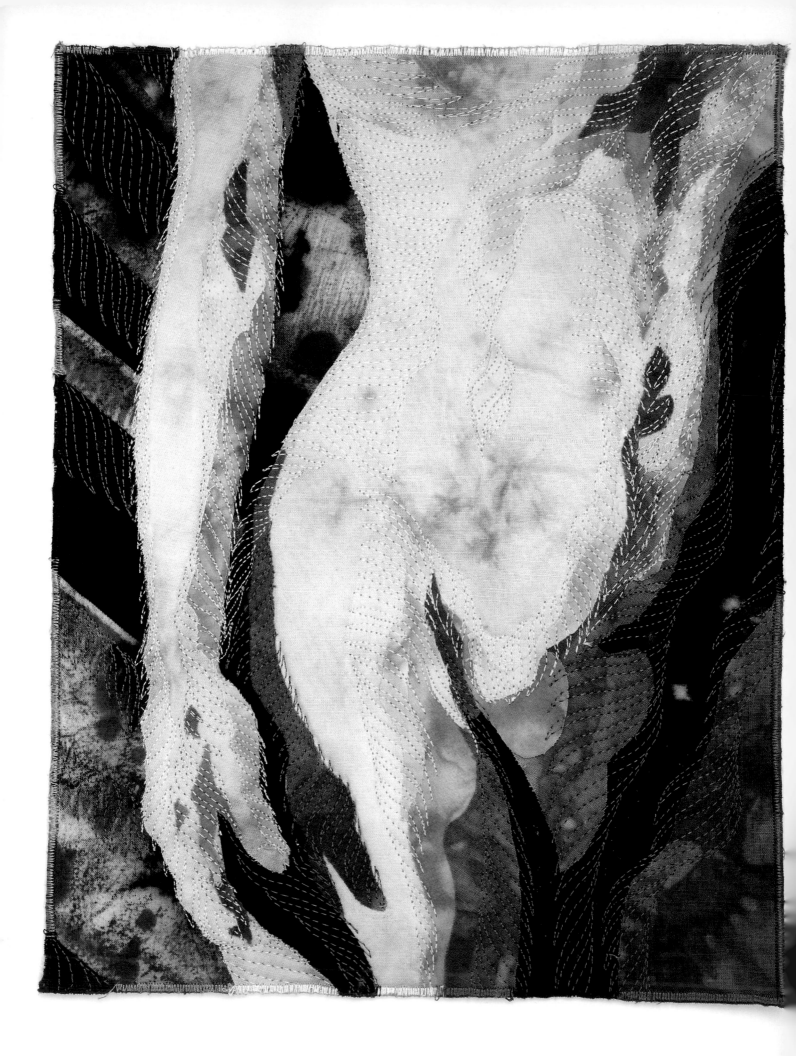

Creative Quilting: THE JOURNAL QUILT PROJECT

Elizabeth Poole
GARRISON, NEW YORK

January 2006 (Opposite)

"The year begins with a self-portrait in acid tones, as true of the artist in January as a red portrait might be in August. Flashes of spring green punctuate the composition, but the heavy hand of winter dominates the color way. All fabrics are hand-dyed; monoprinting, bleach discharge, and raw-edge appliqué were all used. I cropped a digital photo and converted it to grayscale. I then printed it out and began to draw on it, subdividing the photographic image into discrete areas by eye. I traced these areas onto artist's vellum, which I use like a standard sewing pattern. I rely more on instinct than plan to select the fabric for any given area."

Sarah Ann Smith
CAMDEN, MAINE

September 2004 (Top right)

"Maria Elkins' 2003 journals explored faces in various colors and quilting styles. Then, someone on the QuiltArt list suggested we ought to include a self-portrait in our journal quilts, since we mostly know each other only online, not by sight. Taking these as my cue, I used a manipulated digital photo of myself and quilted it in lime, green, and golden yellow. Holding my very basic digital camera at arm's length, I took a picture of myself. In Photoshop® I manipulated this to turn it into a black-and-white image and printed the photo onto pre-treated cotton fabric. With Maria's September QuiltPage showing Bethany with green skin and purple hair in mind, I selected three different shades of green to quilt the face, then a purple, a plum, and a golden yellow thread to quilt my hair."

Michele M.A. David, MD
CHESTNUT HILL, MASSACHUSETTS

February 2005 (Right)

"I decided to explore portraiture for these journal quilts. I wanted to use the machine as a drawing tool and create the effect of a drawing done in charcoal pencil. It was a long, long winter in Massachusetts; the snow kept coming. Doing the journal quilt kept the stress of the winter away. I drew the image on paper from a photograph. Then I made an 8" x 11" mirror copy of the drawing. I pinned this to the back of the fabric and followed the contour of the face and its features. Using free-motion quilting, I then threadpainted the hair and brows."

Elin Waterston
SOUTH SALEM, NEW YORK
April 2002 (Left)

"Here is my husband David on his April birthday when he was about eight or nine years old. To create this piece, I started with a photo-transferred image of my husband as a little boy. I then built the scene around this image, continuing and extending the lines of the background elements, beyond the photograph itself, using commercial fabrics and thread work. This is called photo expansion."

Karol Kusmaul
INVERNESS, FLORIDA
April 2005 (Bottom left)

"In March, a nine-year-old girl in a nearby town was abducted and murdered. Compelled to make a journal quilt about children, I found it difficult to address the evil of what had happened. This April QuiltPage is a generic piece about children; the purple bow in the girl's hair represents the purple stuffed dolphin that the girl took with her when she was abducted from her bedroom. Later, in August, my QuiltPage depicted the girl in an egg shape, representing the fragility and precious nature of children."

Geraldine Congdon
PORTLAND, OREGON
August 2003 (Opposite)

"Bubbly Mia"

"I photographed my granddaughter blowing bubbles and wanted to print the photo with an ethereal feel. In Photoshop®, I manipulated the photo by changing it to grayscale, then to a bitmap image (rows of pixels), and then printed it in sepia tones on dupioni silk treated with Bubble Jet Set®. I machine-appliquéd bubbles of metallic silk organza and added more in the quilting. I used colored pencils to add color to the hair, eyes, bottle, and wand."

Creative Quilting: THE JOURNAL QUILT PROJECT

Cissy Wilson
RICHMOND, TEXAS

April 2005 (Opposite)

"A Face of Faces"

"My daughter-in-law took pictures of all the kids at my grandson's school. We photo-transferred them to make three quilts for a school fundraiser. There were 36 pictures left over. I got the idea of making one child from 36! This face is a composite of parts of all those children. For example, the mouth is made up of the mouths of eight kids, six children's eyes form the eyes here, the ears consist of the ears of four kids, and the nose is made of the noses of nine kids. Thirteen kids' heads also appear. I added French-knot freckles, plus yarn hair, teeth, and eyebrows."

Kathy Lichtendahl
CLARK, WYOMING

January 2004 (Above)

"Two-Faced: Age"

"My 2004 Journal Quilts were all part of a series called 'Two-Faced' based on the premise that none of us is one-dimensional. 'Two-Faced: Age' shows both ends in the spectrum of life. As you approach the quilt from the left, you see the face of youth; as you leave on the right, you can look back and view the face of age. I sketched a rough picture of my father-in-law, who is 80-plus, and another of my two-year-old niece, each on a piece of $8\frac{1}{2}$" x 11" paper. I then drew lines vertically every $\frac{1}{2}$" and cut the drawing into strips that I pasted onto another piece of 17" x 11" paper, placing the strips $\frac{1}{2}$" apart. I filled in the lines and used these horizontally elongated drawings as my patterns to make the two faces out of fabric. I did the quilting, and then I went back into the two mini-quilts and cut them apart every inch, vertically, so I had a collection of 1" strips of fabric faces. These I joined together, alternating the face of my father-in-law and that of my niece. Once I had those all sewn together, I had a 17" x 11" quilt that I placed onto another piece of background fabric, made the little tent shapes, and quilted down every second seam line. This resulted in a finished piece that measured $8\frac{1}{2}$" x 11"."

Deirdre Abbotts
WESTPORT, CONNECTICUT

June 2005

"In May of 2004 I started working on my largest art quilt to date. 'Pandora' was going to be a really big girl. The design progressed quickly, but unfortunately I developed a chronic sinus infection, and the lack of fresh air really hindered the time I could spend making art. I was frustrated at not being able to regain my health, despite getting medical care right away. For what seemed like months, I worked on different parts of the quilt. I decided to use Angelina® for the spirits leaving Pandora's Box and purchased many colors of gold and white Angelina® and Tintzl. After months of fooling around with them, I decided they were too bright and reworked my idea. Pandora's image in this QuiltPage is a photograph that I took of my original painting. She was printed on cotton fabric using DURABrite® inks. The Spirits swirling around Pandora deceive us into thinking that they are benevolent. Too late we find that what appears innocent can be deadly. To convey the Spirits, I layered the remnants from the Angelina® and Tintzl that were originally going to be used on the full-size quilt under a sheer covering of tulle."

Marion Coleman
CASTRO VALLEY, CALIFORNIA

May 2004

"After 20 years of wearing my hair short, I decided to let it grow. This is my portrait with short locks. I took a digital photo of myself, then I used the Photoshop® Elements threshold feature to change the photo to black-and-white. The photo was printed onto cotton treated with Bubble Jet Set®; additional fabrics were added to the photo, machine-quilted, and bound with the backing."

Jeri Riggs
DOBBS FERRY, NEW YORK

September 2003

"My Evil Muse reappears, disguised in a blue dress. I've used this image in previous quilts, and here she is drawn right onto the fabric. She still emerges as herself, barbs and all. I made a line drawing of the woman on paper, and then traced the drawing onto batik fabric. I colored it in with fabric markers and layered and quilted over the design lines with black cotton thread."

Gloria Hansen
HIGHTSTOWN, NEW JERSEY

January 2003

"Princess Pixel Pusher"

"That's me and the name I gave myself after the realization that I spend a good part of my day using Photoshop® to create designs, repair and enhance photos, etc. Although I enjoy my work, one day I exclaimed, 'I am a pixel pusher; I am Princess Pixel Pusher!' I created the design for this quilt starting with a photograph of myself. I selected certain areas of the photo and reduced them to pixel-like squares using the mosaic filter in Photoshop®. Since I didn't want to be entirely swallowed up by pixels, I masked out some of them to bring in features from the original photograph. It is printed on cotton and machine-quilted. There are untouched areas—my way of saying, 'I'm still here!'"

Creative Quilting: THE JOURNAL QUILT PROJECT

Synnøve Vånar

HVALSTAD, NORWAY

July 2005 (Opposite)

"Erling"

"I wanted to make a portrait quilt, and it was not as difficult as I had expected. I started out painting fabric for the face. White, black, yellow, and red combine to make skin color. Uneven painting gives a good basic foundation, because of the light coming from one direction. I copied a photo of our son Erling to the size I needed and traced the outlines onto tracing paper. I moved the paper over the painted surface and then pinned it onto the fabric where I found a good spot with light and dark. I sewed on the paper along the drawn lines and then removed the paper. The hair I tried to cut in organic forms, thinking light and dark. Holes for the eyes were cut out. The eyes were made separately and zigzagged on. I zigzagged all the pieces with multi-colored thread, while moving the fabric a little to make it look organic. I cut out the face, and sewed it on to a suitable background fabric. The outline of the nose was made by putting two contrasting threads in the needle and making big stitches. The mouth was cut out and put on. At last, tulle in different colors was put on the face where the shadows (or light) were and sewn on with invisible thread. I learned this technique from Solvejg Refslund, Denmark, in a workshop called Picture Sewing."

March 2004 (Top right)

"Will I make it to the top?"

"In March I went skiing with a group in the Norwegian mountains for a week, carrying everything I needed in a rucksack. A wonderful week! The last day our leader invited some of the men to join him on a trip to the mountaintop, Store Svuku. Eager to go, I joined without being asked. This QuiltPage was inspired by a picture taken of me before we started."

Phyllis A. Cullen

CHICO, CALIFORNIA

January 2006 (Right)

"In January I took a workshop on creating faces in thread with Cheryl Bridgart. After years of sketching people with a pencil, I found that it was easy and fun to sketch them directly with a sewing needle, using various thread colors. No need for appliqué, painting, or drawing first! Here I used free-motion machine embroidery (threadpainting) done freehand on blank, non-woven, medium-weight stabilizer machine-appliquéd to silk, with a machine-appliquéd 'frame'."

Kris A. Bishop
WOODBRIDGE, VIRGINIA

August 2003

"Life Line"

"I was born with a birthmark in the palm of my left hand. I have always been fascinated by it. As I have aged, it has gotten paler in color, but I have always believed that it brought me good luck. This is from my self-portrait series. I scanned the palm of my left hand into my computer and then printed it out on pre-treated fabric sheets. I cut out the scanned hand and machine-appliquéd it to a background fabric. I also added a watch face to represent my watch, which always seems to slide around backwards, and then machine-quilted my 'life lines' and the background."

Sharon K. Gipson
DECATUR, GEORGIA

January 2006

"This page represents my 2006 resolution to avoid getting so caught up in the rat race that I don't enjoy the finer things in life like family, friends, and creating. The hand-dyed background fabric looks like a spider's web to me. The shape representing me caught in the web is raw-edged appliqué. The slightly frayed edges show how I feel when I am all caught up in stressful situations. I used machine straight-stretch stitches for my hair and the web."

Pamela Reilly
HOBOKEN, NEW JERSEY
January 2006

"A return to quilting after 14 years (divorce, remarriage, birth, death, and illness) is no small triumph. This piece was roughly and quickly put together; I didn't want to hide the process. It includes Polaroid transfers I did for my last exhibit in 1992. This piece comes from someplace which has no words, pulling together what I knew then with who I am now."

Kimberly Hamilton
LOWER SACKVILLE,
NOVA SCOTIA, CANADA
February 2005

"I was given a small Inuksuk as a gift in 2001 before my first move. It has had a place of honor in every one of my five homes since. The Inuksuk is an Inuit symbol often seen in the Canadian North and is used to guide lost travelers home. For me, this quilt is about unknown journeys, new directions, unforeseen events, and finding the path home. After three years, I am home...a new home, but home none the less."

Creative Quilting: THE JOURNAL QUILT PROJECT

Cay Denise MacKenzie
SUNNYVALE, CALIFORNIA

June 2004 (Opposite)

"Vintage Pastel"

"My June QuiltPage is a rescued mistake and a first attempt at using a printer to print a photograph on silk chiffon. The problem was in setting the print. After steaming, multiple blue 'blobs' appeared on the fabric. So, I added a blue batik fabric behind the silk to camouflage the blobs' intensity and then painted over the problem areas. The stitching emphasizes elements of the photograph."

September 2005 (Right)

"This is a fun self-portrait! This piece started out as a simple pencil drawing that was cut up and used as templates. The hat has a veil and floral pin embellishing it. The big earrings are made of decorated polymer clay. The template pieces were fused to a background fabric and satin-stitched. Echo quilting finished the piece."

Shirley Jo Rimkus-Falconer
INDEPENDENCE, OREGON

January 2006 (Right)

"I'm going to make it my personal goal to do a face a month, each one using a different technique. My first is a girl; the technique is raw-edge appliqué and fusing. She is fused with Steam-A-Seam 2 Lite®, then randomly quilted by machine, except for her face."

Luana Rubin

BOULDER, COLORADO

June 2003 (Left)

"On this month's QuiltPage, I took scraps from my Bernina Fashion Show garment and my Sweet Stuff collection for Kaufman Fabrics to make a portrait page of Sophie, my adopted daughter. I took this photo of her at the White Swan Hotel in Guangzhou, China, and she is dressed in pink silk pajamas with embroidery and soutache. Red is the most auspicious color for the Chinese people, and so as I make this portrait, it is intended as a blessing—a prayer for her health and happiness in our family and in this country. The Chinese silk brocade under the photo, and also the silk velvet burnout fabric around the photo, were sculpturally draped and stitched down to give the illusion of depth. The portrait was free-motion quilted with copper metallic thread."

Mary-Ellen Latino

SOUTHBOROUGH, MASSACHUSETTS

May 2004 (Bottom left)

"Celebrating the Journey"

"This QuiltPage documents two of my three sons graduating this month: Justin from St. John's High School and Jesse from Ithaca College. They are each celebrating their accomplishments, dancing at the tree of knowledge, the tree of life. As they continue the journey they'll reach for the moon and catch many stars along the way. This piece also depicts the abundant love and pride the artist has for her sons! I free-motion, machine-embroidered the tree with variegated threads using Solvy™ stabilizer. I then fused this onto the hand-dyed, discharged, and over-dyed silk noil background. The figures were hand-dyed, metallic-painted, and fused onto the background. The words and stars were fused onto fabric and foiled with different colors. The moon was created using pearlescent paint. I used hand-sewn beads as embellishment."

Linda S. Schmidt

DUBLIN, CALIFORNIA

April 2005 (Opposite)

"The Kiss"

"While in Minnesota for a wedding, I saw a lovely photograph that my brother-in-law, Buddy Ferguson, had taken of family and friends. Here is my sister Gloria with her daycare child, Cole, and two friends, Amber and Mary, in the park. Given permission, I used the photograph to make two large-scale quilts of the scene—one for Gloria's office and one for myself. Using Setacolor fabric paints, I painted this miniature version of the center of that quilt. I traced the photo onto tracing paper and then traced that onto PFD fabric using Pigma® fine markers. I painted the whole scene with transparent fabric paints, then appliquéd the people with invisible thread."

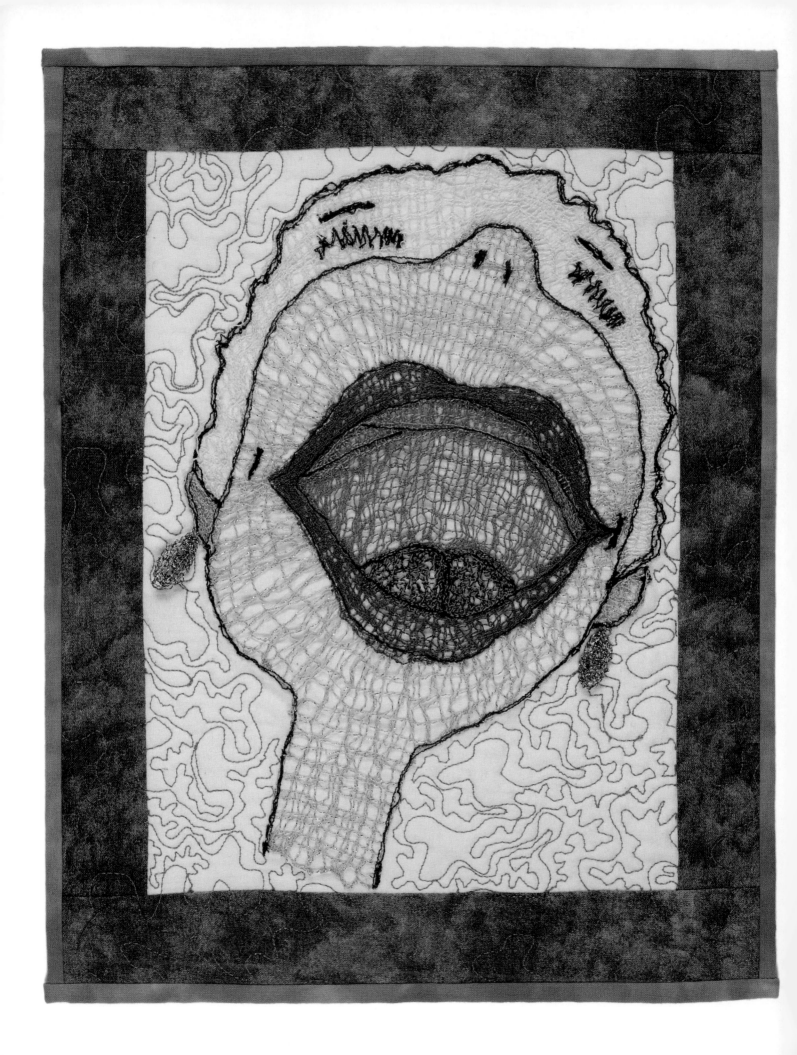

Creative Quilting: THE JOURNAL QUILT PROJECT

Judith McIrvin
CHANTILLY, VIRGINIA

March 2003 (Opposite)

"The March self-portrait was a response to feeling some brief relief from difficult winter weather and painful physical therapy. I was elated to be able to work at my art, and especially that I could once more use my right leg to press the sewing machine pedal. I drew my face on thick water-soluble stabilizer; then I used cotton, polyester, and metallic threads and machine-embroidered onto the stabilizer on top of cotton fabric. After dissolving the stabilizer, the ink disappeared, leaving only the embroidery on the cotton background. The embroidered earrings were left hanging loose."

Patty Gamburg
ALEXANDRIA, LOUISIANA

May 2005 (Top right)

"This is the fifth in a series of journal quilts entitled 'Women in My Life.' It is a caricature representing my Aunt Jessie Matthews, my mother's older sister. She was a nurse and influenced me to become a nurse."

Francie Gass
BELLINGHAM, WASHINGTON

May 2003 (Right)

"Every spring I struggle between wanting a lovely garden and wanting to spend my time inside sewing. This is me, dreaming of quilting as I'm drowning in weeds. The 'weed' fabric is hand-dyed by Sarah Smith. I fused it and the knit face and hands fabric and zigzagged the edges. Fabric pens were used to draw the face and fingers. The hair is done with free-motion quilting."

Mary E. McBride
DELAND, FLORIDA

January 2005

"Pandora and Her Box of Tricks"

"Helen Howell enticed me with her experience, ranging from painting fabric to metal smithing. She always has something new to teach, but every time she opens that box of hers, I become involved in a new passion. She has touched me, believed in me, taught me, praised me, and chastised me for not having confidence in my own voice. Now I'm putting her face in a book! Working in Photoshop®, I used a filter to turn Helen's face into a patchwork image, adjusted the colors to her favorite blues, and enlarged the image of both her face and the triangular box she is holding. Then I printed both items on untreated fabric. (At first, I had printed Helen in Tyvek® but melted it with the iron, a hard lesson to learn.) The sheet of copper was cut into a strip, run through a crimper, folded and twisted, then run through the crimper again. Finally, I used pliers to hand-crimp the curves."

Meena Schaldenbrand
PLYMOUTH, MICHIGAN

March 2004

"Portrait of Albert Einstein"

"This QuiltPage is a thread-sketched, sewing-machine portrait of one of the most famous people in history. I obtained the copyright-free illustration from READY-TO-USE PORTRAITS OF FAMOUS PEOPLE and printed it on tracing paper. I layered the fabric wrong-side up, added the batting, and finally, the portrait. I placed the resulting sandwich on the sewing machine with the paper-side up, fabric-side down. I set the stitch length and width to zero and pulled the bottom thread to the top. I then free-motion embroidered the face with brown thread and removed the tracing paper when the portrait was complete."

Kathy Nida

EL CAJON, CALIFORNIA

May 2005

"Thinking about that whole woman-as-vessel thing, I wish I could turn a switch and no longer be fertile. I worry that there are three arrows out of my womb, but I only have two children at the moment. I don't think I could handle having more babies at this late stage, but my body refuses to shut the flow off. It thinks it's too early. I don't really know what I want."

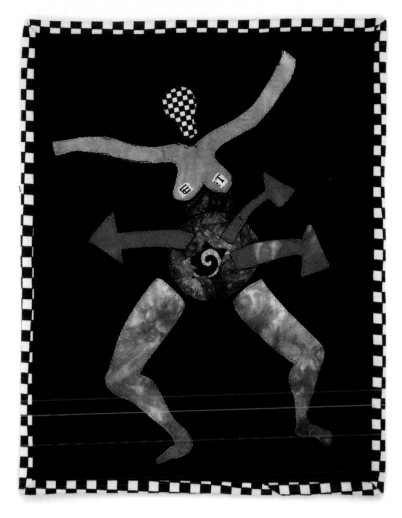

Anne Holliday-Abbott

PORTLAND, MAINE

January 2006

"In early January my daughter Marcia and I hosted our art history group, and the teapot was the focal point of our wintry gathering. The self-portrait behind the teapot shows me inspired by our discussion of Byzantine art. This is the first time I have sketched on a QuiltPage, and I was very happy with the results. Hand-painted muslin was used along with embellishments of tulle, buttons, beads, and crocheted medallions."

Mary Louise Smith

BROOKLYN, NEW YORK

March 2002 (Left)

"My theme was in response to coping and recovering from a devastating illness. Utilizing different quilting techniques challenged my creativity. It was the support of my quilting friends that was helpful in motivating me to overcome my feelings of helplessness during that time. They gave me the courage to continue to quilt. This was my first redwork embroidery piece. This original design I created reflects the bond of quilting sisterhood that I felt."

April 2004 (Bottom left)

"My Autumn Muse"

"In stretching my creativity, I incorporated theme fabrics with fabric painting in the form of my nude muses (original design) to convey the seasons and nature. 'My Autumn Muse' is set against a background fabric that epitomizes the fall season. Her stylized green hair is a contrast against the background."

Susan Ossana

MOAB, UTAH

January 2006 (Opposite)

"My identical twin granddaughters, Bianca and Portia, couldn't have possibly arrived by anything as ordinary as a stork—flamingos are more their style! My daughter, Autumn, is upside down, and I might as well be— twins are a handful! The quilt is hand-appliquéd and hand-embroidered with a buttonhole stitch."

Vicki C. Mangum
KATY, TEXAS

January 2006

"Sheri"

"Ever since learning Sheri has cancer, I have been thinking of her constantly. Her surgery is tomorrow, and I must create something. I found this wonderful image that reminded me of her beauty and individuality. I used a photo fabric print, embellished with an iron-on Swarovski crystal as a beauty mark and hand-sewn beads as a band on the head-covering. Gold beads were added by hand to the striped fabric. This was the first time I used Angelina® fibers—great embellishment!"

Leslie Tucker Jenison
SAN ANTONIO, TEXAS

August 2002

"Reunion"

"Attending my 30th high school class reunion was a very poignant experience. I returned to my hometown accompanied by my oldest daughter Lauren. We were on a road trip that included spending time with my mother, whose fragile health indicated that this might be the last time my daughter, who attends school in the northeast, would see her grandmother. Lauren attended my reunion, and we discussed the many differences between her high school experience and mine, 29 years apart. My QuiltPage attempts to combine thoughts and imagery from the years 1969 through 1972; these were my high school years. I printed the text onto a transparency, then layered photos and other imagery behind the transparency and scanned them onto cotton fabric."

Debbie Bates

NEWMARKET, ONTARIO, CANADA

September 2005

"Finding True North"

"We each have our own destination in the stars. Inspiration shows us the one star we should fly towards. Wow, the final entry in this year's series turned out to be a celebration of completing my challenge and of self-discovery. I knew the bones of this story when I began the journey, but I had no expectations of truly discovering anything. To do the work would have been enough. Instead, I was pleasantly surprised to find my style in these stitches. It's pure me—derriere, gray hair, secret wings, and all! I outlined the figure lightly in pencil on flesh-toned fabric and then added layers of colored pencil highlights using the side rather than the point of the pencil. I then blended the colors by rubbing with a fingertip."

Ann Louise Mullard-Pugh

LAS VEGAS, NEVADA

May 2002

"As I fly back and forth to Virginia to visit my Mom at her nursing home and my sister Emilie, I remember an old folk tale...that somewhere in time, women could fly. We probably gave it up as it ruined our hair and we got tired of picking bugs out of our teeth. It might still be worth it if it meant we could avoid the hassle of modern airports. I used sun-printed fabric, hand metallic embroidery, and appliqué."

6: Faces & Figures

Creative Quilting: THE JOURNAL QUILT PROJECT

Gwen Maxwell-Williams
REDMOND, WASHINGTON

March 2005 (Opposite)

"Another maiden in this series—this is probably my favorite. She is very peaceful, very serene. Surrounded by flowers, she needed beads to complete the scene. Fusing, raw-edge appliqué, and beads were used, along with images from Julia Cairns' Maasai Maidens fabric collection."

Sharie Myers
ANN ARBOR, MICHIGAN

March 2005 (Top right)

"Trying to find balance in my work, family, and play was a big-ticket item for me in 2005. I used 'balance' as a theme for several paper collages, choosing one to convert from paper to fabric for this QuiltPage. I used black fabric as a background on which I had written with a silver fabric pen something about a self-help television show I had seen on television. The figure, plates, shapes, and words were raw-edge appliquéd. I wanted a strong focal point in this piece, because it is not my usual style. I chose a triangle on-point for the base for the figure to give a sense of instability and tension. One of the spinning plates had fallen showing that nothing is perfect, including this piece. The design and construction of this piece was influenced and inspired by all I've learned over the last few years from fiber and collage artists such as Susan Shie, Claudine Hellmuth, Teesha and Tracy Moore, Kristi Schueler, Molly Bang, and many other artists who share their visual creations with the world."

Patricia C. Dolan
MANALAPAN, NEW JERSEY

February 2006 (Right)

"Symbolically, this time of my life (retirement) marks the ending of my own Mardi Gras—the end of roles, masks, and illusions—as I step forward into the freedom of personal authenticity and truth. The experimental process using Shiva® Paintstiks® over stamps on my Setacolor painted chiffon symbolizes the patterns of my life up to now. The heads with fly-away hair symbolize the masks and roles that are now falling away. I rubbed the Paintstiks (à la Laura Murray) over my grandmother's old metal cookie mold and a foam spiral to create the background patterns. For the clay heads, I discovered that Pearl-Ex® pigments rubbed and/or gently pressed into the clay prior to drying/baking created a marvelous iridescent glow."

Denise A. Hitzfield
ROANOKE, INDIANA

August 2005 (Left)

"Knock It Off! A Self-portrait"

"After severe disappointment, self-realization and reflection become overpowering. This produces a sense of being out-of-control, constantly thinking of past mistakes, with a focus on the future mysteries of my life."

Marilyn League
MEMPHIS, TENNESSEE

January 2006 (Bottom left)

"Dreams seemed like the most obvious subject for my journal quilts, as I have had some amazing and strange dreams since childhood. Some of my dreams are like movies, and there are other dreams that nag at me all the next day, begging for explanation. I think the best way to deal with all of them is to get them out of my head and into a physical form. The viewer of these 'dream quilts' can then be entertained by the images or make her own guess as to their meanings. Some of the QuiltPages of this journal will be images from recent dreams, ones that have been particularly interesting. Others will be inspired by past dreams that I'm keeping in a mental archive. This dream was of the movie category and was quite entertaining. It was a cross between INVASION OF THE BODY SNATCHERS and delivery of the new yellow pages. I was experimenting with inset piecing techniques from Dale Fleming's book, PIECED CURVES, SO SIMPLE, so I pieced together the background and then inserted the yellow people. I have done lots of pieced curves over the years, but before I always had to make a pattern of the entire quilt. This new technique allows for more freedom of placement within the design."

Cynthia Paugh St. Charles
BILLINGS, MONTANA

January 2006 (Opposite)

"Lady in Waiting"

"The swelling belly of my pregnant daughter Elizabeth inspired this prototype for a larger quilt. I loved the lines of an Egyptian tomb painting of a seated female figure, and wanted to use that style for this piece. The background fabric was hand-dyed using the low-water immersion technique. The female figure was my first attempt at hand marbling fabrics. CREATIVE MARBLING ON FABRIC: A GUIDE TO MAKING ONE-OF-A-KIND FABRICS by Judy Simmons was my guide for this first experiment. Fabrics must be pre-treated. Marbling colors are dropped onto the marbling base in a shallow tray and then raked to create the distinctive marbling design. Once you are satisfied with the pattern, the fabric is carefully lowered onto the tray. The marbled design is transferred to the fabric."

CHAPTER 6: FACES & FIGURES

Lauralyn Sciretta
TUCSON, ARIZONA

January 2003 (Opposite)

"I hand-dyed the sky fabric, and for the rock shadows used the reverse side of fabric. I chose a rock climber image to capture January as being the time when we try to set resolutions and goals. I resorted to using dye pens for small features; in a larger format I would do all appliqué. I had cut some small pieces for the shoe for instance, but it was just too small to handle—like trying to write your name on rice. I love that fabric I used on her tights; I want a pair!"

Priscilla Stultz
FAIRFAX, VIRGINIA

February 2002 (Top right)

"My sewing studio is the place where I spend most of my time. The passion for fabric manipulation has been part of my life since childhood. The scissors, thread, fabric, and needle in my hands become an extension of myself, a feeling that brings me joy and contentment. Each creation becomes part of me, and I leave part of myself in each creation. I am a spontaneous designer and rarely pre-plan my projects. This QuiltPage contains Sashiko stitching, a primitive stitching used in 18th century Japan to patch indigo garments. The Sashiko stitch is similar to a hand running stitch. Diaper flannel is used as the batting layer. The designs are from a miniature quilting design stencil, drawn with a pencil to the flannel side of the project; the design is stitched from the flannel side and a backing added."

Necia Wallace
WHITEFISH BAY, WISCONSIN

June 2002 (Right)

"The first year, the Journal Quilt Project urged experimentation, so in my first five months, I experimented with acrylic paints. In May I painted a Chinese opera mask; masks intrigue me as they alter the viewer's perception. For June I printed out five reduced images of the same mask and printed the resulting petal design on yellow fabric. I think I should have heightened the color saturation when I printed the masks, and perhaps orange would have been better for the background fabric. That's what experimenting is all about."

Louisa L. Smith
LOVELAND, COLORADO

March 2005 (Left)

"I created this QuiltPage using a simplified digital self-image taken in color, printed in black-and-white, modified, and interpreted in fabric. It was fused and machine-stitched. I placed threads under netting that I then machine-embroidered to the top and fused dupioni silk pieces to the design. By giving myself permission to 'go outside the lines,' I discovered the limitless possibilities quilting offers and the liberating feeling that comes from taking advantage of this. I want my quilts to spark the imagination of the people who view them, to help see the world in new ways, to sing with color...and above all, to be pleasing to the eye!"

Bobbie Vance
LAFAYETTE, INDIANA

January 2006 (Bottom left)

"Beading in PV, MX"

"In the middle of January '06 I spent a week in Puerto Vallarta, Mexico, at a fabulous artsy B&B—Hacienda Mosaico. I was there to study beading on a loom with Don Pierce and 13 fun people. I wanted to do a mosaic QuiltPage to represent my trip. I started the mosaic with the sky, using a hand-painted silk jacquard, and the rest of the QuiltPage developed from two simplified pictures I took of the place we stayed. Yes, my hair was partially purple (on purpose) while there. And my hand-dyed skin color? Well, there was more than once that the group helped fan those darn hot flashes...The face is actually a mini-quilt with batting and backing, attached to the main QuiltPage only by the eyes."

Lura Schwarz Smith
COARSEGOLD, CALIFORNIA

May 2004 (Opposite)

"Staples"

"Completely unexpectedly and inconveniently, I find myself in the hospital with major surgery to remove an intestinal tumor. At least the doctors wear scenic purple gloves—but I'm not so wild about all the staples up my belly. I learn that everything can be rescheduled as necessary, after all. 'Staples' are the theme of this month. I hand-painted the base fabric with textile paints, then fused fabrics to this. Real purple latex surgeon's gloves and my hospital I.D. wristband were machine-stitched down. I machine-quilted it and then stapled 17 times right through everything to match the number of staples I had after the surgery."

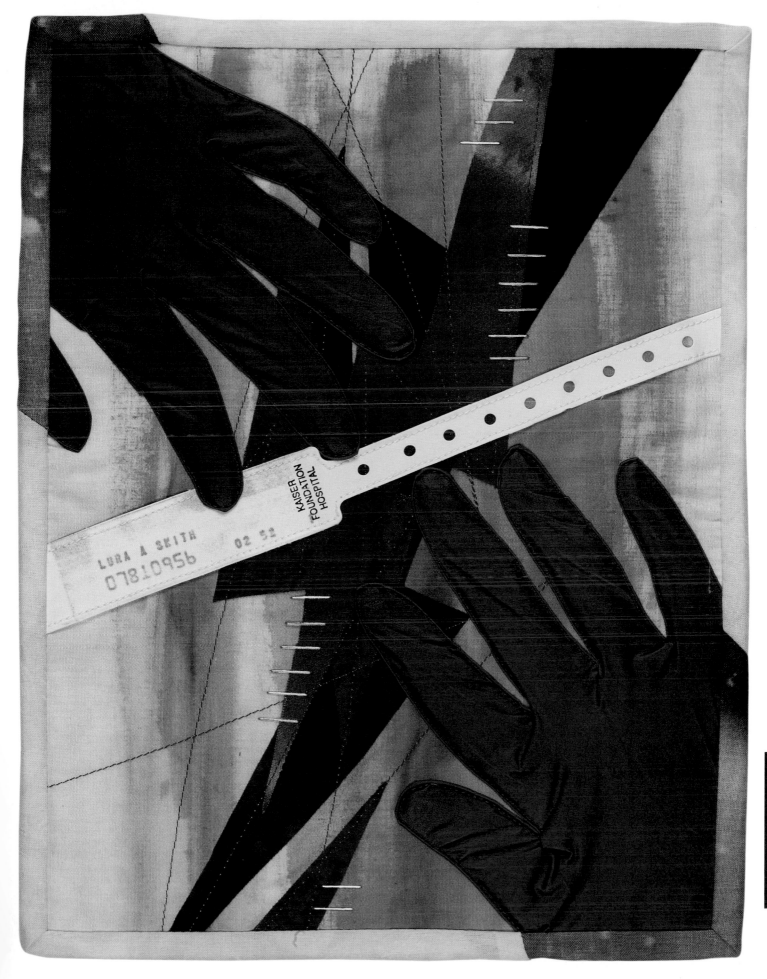

Els Vereycken
HASSELT, BELGIUM

January 2004

"This is a bust of my son Ivo and is the first page of my Journal Quilt. The same bust is turned in all directions for all the other months. I took pictures of the bust in all the different directions and then created a drawing with special accents, which helped me to choose the hand-dyed fabric."

Maria V. Weinstein
NEW CITY, NEW YORK

January 2006

"I wanted to start the year taking a closer look at myself, in plain or not-so-plain fabric. Lime green, dragonflies, and sunflowers are all part of me. Hair is nearly always wild, so to create it, I used loose threads pulled out of my vacuum, placed on fusible, and trimmed. Most of the time, my eyes are wide open to take in all learning opportunities around me. I love wearing big earrings. Sometimes I hate my full lips. However, knowing that women now pay plenty for full lips, I've learned to love them!"

Abstract

It is a common misconception that abstract art— non-representational, non-figurative art in which the artist expresses himself purely through the use of form and color—is a 20th century invention. In fact, it can be traced back through the centuries to the Jewish and Islamic religions, both of which forbade artists and sculptors to depict human beings. This prohibition resulted in the development of a high standard of non-figurative art by these cultures, particularly in calligraphy and in patterns for textiles and pottery. However, some experts credit Wassily Kandinsky as the inventor of this movement, since it was he who, in 1910, created a watercolor that was the first completely abstract work of art. This represented a drastic break with the 19th century European idea that art should imitate nature or tell a story.

Among the components of abstract art are a strong emphasis on colors and forms, either geometric or non-geometric; the use of materials as the subject of the art; the use of figurative abstractions, where detail is eliminated from recognizable objects, abstracting or leaving only the essence—perhaps even just a fragment—of recognizable form; the attempt to represent things that are not visual, such as emotion, sound, or spiritual experience; skewed perspective showing several points of view at once; individuality; and treating the whole piece with equal importance (instead of having the center more interesting than the edges, for example). Each of these components can be found in the abstract QuiltPages in this chapter.

As artist Harley Hahn states on his web page: "The more abstract a work of art, the less preconceptions it evokes in the mind of the beholder...The reason abstract art has the potential to be so powerful is that it keeps the conscious distractions to a minimum... When you look at [an abstract painting] you are not distracted by meaningful images, so virtually all of your brain power is devoted to feeling. You can open yourself, let in the energy and spirit of the [art], and allow it to dance with your psyche."

The reader of this chapter will no doubt have a lively jitterbug with his or her psyche, because the Abstract Journal QuiltPages not only run the gamut of emotions but also present many challenging techniques to study.

Creative Quilting: THE JOURNAL QUILT PROJECT

Heidi Lund

BREMERTON, WASHINGTON

(This page and opposite)

July 2002 (Opposite)

"July was the month to work on cleaning up my studio. Having just finished my fishy Bernina® Fashion Show ensemble, I could not bring myself to toss all those little fabric scraps out. Instead I rotary-cut up all kinds of scraps: cotton, tulle, silk noil, and satin. I covered it in a water-soluble stabilizer and free-motion machine-stitched all over the top. After rinsing out the stabilizer, I gathered scraps of curly edged ombre ribbon and made little 'nests' for beads to hide in. With the addition of beads and buttons embellished with beads, it was a great use of scraps!"

March 2003 (Top right)

"Orange Sherbet"

"This quilt started as a challenge to myself to use that orange sherbet-colored fabric at a time when I kept seeing forests in California raging in orange flames and smoke. I experimented with applying Lumiere® metallic paint with a sponge brush to a stamp shaped like a tree, then stamping the tree onto the fabric. I fused small, pointed shapes and appliquéd them for flames. In the middle of the piece, I felt it needed a drastic change. I took all kinds of shimmery, sheer fabric scraps, whacked them up with my rotary cutter, and dropped them haphazardly on the quilt. I laid a piece of Solvy™ over everything and stitched away. After rinsing out the water-soluble stabilizer, I really liked the raw edges. This piece features free-motion machine threadwork, appliqué, and sequins and beads for dimension and embellishment."

August 2002 (Right)

"August was the month I challenged myself to take a beautiful piece of printed cloth and use only thread as my paintbrush. To do my freeform threadpainting, I used several different colors of Sulky® rayon threads and tried out a new thread on the market called Holoshimmer®. After completing this quilt, I decided that it would be a good inspiration to make a vest using the same technique, possibly out of one of those fabrics that I have been hoarding for years and could not bring myself to cut. Twisted fibers were whip-stitched around the outside edge for a new take on bindings."

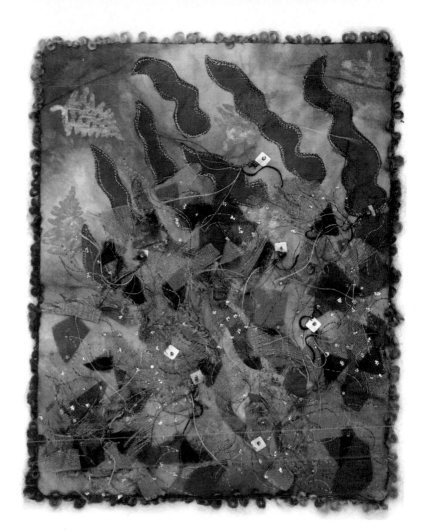

Brenda Tower Jennings
COLUMBUS, OHIO

January 2006

"In response to both a minor health issue that had me feeling down and a nagging quilt project that was bogging me down, my January QuiltPage is not only about fear and feeling 'trapped' but also about finding the light at the end of the tunnel. The fabrics are from a new project I started working on at the time, and the light area in the center is to represent the beginnings of freedom: freedom to create; freedom to work on things that I want to do; freedom to get my old self back. I fused fabric scraps to Timtex™ using raw-edge appliqué and used mostly Asian-patterned cottons."

Linda McLaughlin
WEISER, IDAHO

January 2006

"My Journal Quilts for this year will all contain a piece of hand-painted, pink-and-orange fabric that was formerly the cover on my print table. January's QuiltPage is based on a quote from Charles Shultz: 'Life is like a ten-speed bike; we all have gears we never use.' Using two sizes of copies of a gear, I used Citra-Solv® to transfer some faint gear images onto the background. Then I made Thermofax® screens of the gear and printed them onto the fabric. I wrote the quote with a fabric pen."

Catherine Kleeman

RUXTON, MARYLAND • *July 2003*

"I have always visualized the months of the year as colors. They range from dull gray and brown during Winter, become vibrant through Spring and Summer, wind down through fall colors, and then return to winter gray. July is the hottest, most humid, and most uncomfortable month. It feels like a red-orange fireball. It's too hot to breathe. Yellows, oranges, reds with hot gold are the colors of July for me. To create the foiled sun, I drew the design freehand with India ink and inked in the image. Since India ink is carbon-based, it will cause a thermal imaging machine to burn the image onto a thermal screen, which can then be used to screen-print. I screened the image with Laura Murray's Foil Transfer Adhesive. Once the adhesive had dried, the gold foil could be ironed onto the fabric to create the sun image."

7: Abstract

Vickie Meredith Lord
ATLANTA, GEORGIA

January 2006 (Left)

"This was my very first journal page and I was feeling a little overwhelmed at the prospect of doing one every month! I was thinking of New Year's resolutions. I thought about just writing 'stop procrastinating,' but that sounded so negative, so I imagined a very positive fortune cookie and this is what I wished for myself. It's brought me very good karma so far!"

Mary Jane Russell
COLCHESTER, VERMONT

February 2006 (Bottom left)

"A QUILTING ARTS MAGAZINE® article about alternative edge finishes inspired me to stitch the backing, batting, and background together first, leaving raw edges instead of using a binding. I collaged hand-painted fabric, African mudcloth, and some of my own handmade Nuno felt (constructed by gently felting merino wool, mohair locks, and embellishments into silk gauze) onto this base. I purposely left loose ends of rayon thread hanging from the front of the quilt—neatened and tied down with beads. This Journal Quilt process is awesome!"

Claire Waguespack Fenton
HOUMA, LOUISIANA

January 2003 (Opposite)

"Window of Opportunity"

"This piece reflects my vision of diving into a new world. Beginning with a section of my hand-dyed fabric, I couched and trapped various threads, silk fibers, and yarns under layers of tulle, leaving the figure near the top edge uncovered. To unify it, and create motion, I machine-stitched a grid work over the rest of the piece. I bound the edges with rolled strips of old silk ties. I begin by tightly twisting each old tie lengthwise. I insert one end under the presser foot, take a few long zigzag stitches to anchor it, and continue twisting and zigzagging along the length of each tie. When I near the end of the first tie, I insert the next one into the twist and zigzag over this joint. The coil will vary in thickness with the width of the tie as well as the fabric: silk is obviously thinner than heavy polyester."

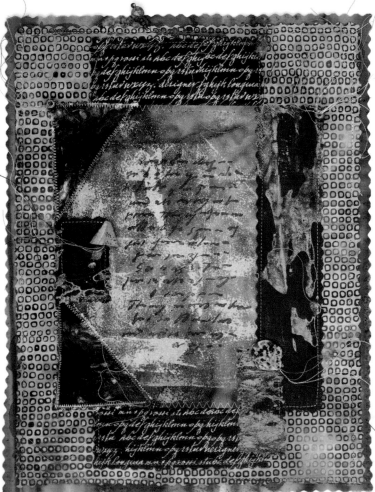

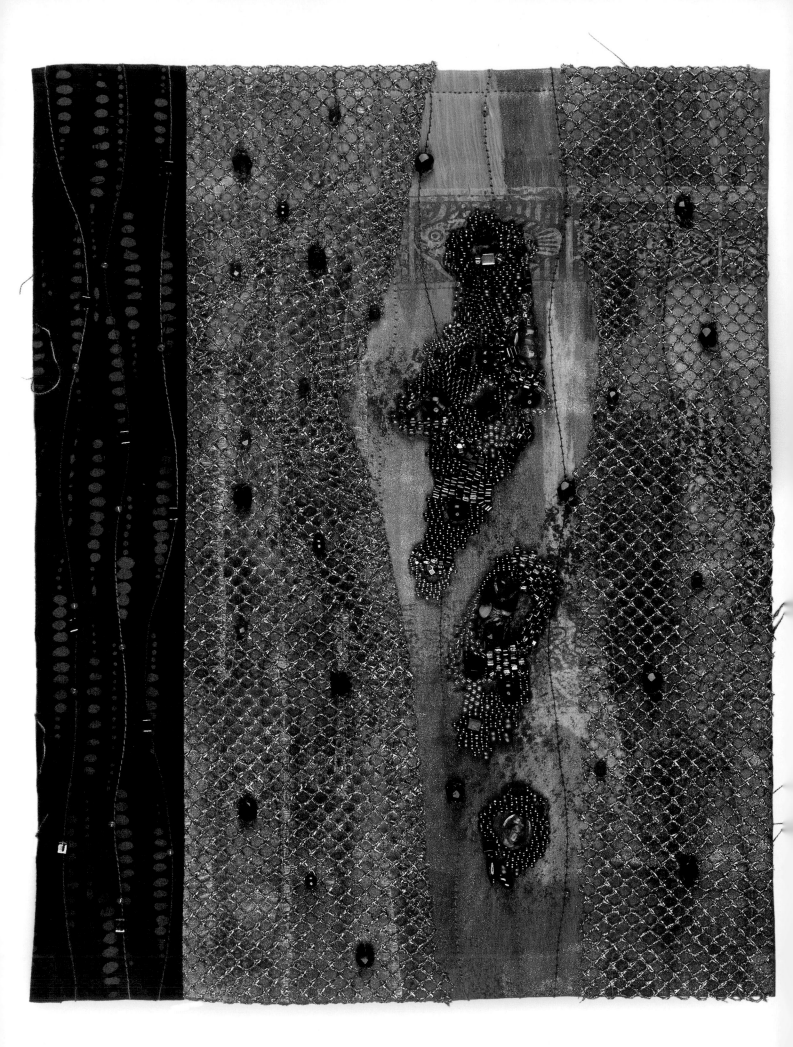

Creative Quilting: THE JOURNAL QUILT PROJECT

Christine Eisenberg

SIMI VALLEY, CALIFORNIA

April 2005 (Opposite)

"Poseidon's Treasure"

"I love the organic look of sculptural peyote, which is a type of seed bead stitch, and since I had wanted to learn this stitch to create embellishments for quilts, I took beading classes. As a result, I discovered that I love beading, and I love combining beading and quilting. The three peyote pieces remind me of jewel-encrusted treasure hidden at the bottom of the sea. I painted and stamped a watery, silky background fabric to imply an undersea setting, then covered it with netting that falls apart to reveal the 'treasure.'"

Katherine Leever

PAMPA, TEXAS

January 2006 (Top right)

"January in the Texas Panhandle is varying shades of beige; the most dominant feature is the sky. This winter everyone is looking at the sky and hoping for precipitation—rain, snow, sleet; we'll take whatever we can get to break this drought. I used hand-dyed fabric, a tulle overlay distressed with a hot iron, and hand-beaded embellishment."

Jenny Perry

WHITLEY CITY, KENTUCKY

January 2006 (Bottom right)

"Inspired by Gillian Hand's work in MAKE YOUR OWN CONTEMPORARY QUILTS, I started a series of experimental quilts using a variation of her faux-felt technique. I used dyed wool and silk roving intended for spinning into yarn. An abstract design was created by pulling these fibers apart and spreading them onto a base of my own hand-painted silk organza. Water-soluble stabilizer held all the fibers in place, and it was machine-quilted heavily. The layers merged into a single felted fabric after immersion in water."

Creative Quilting: THE JOURNAL QUILT PROJECT

Flo Peel

QUALICUM BEACH, BRITISH COLUMBIA, CANADA

July 2002 (Opposite)

"I chose to experiment with silk fusion as the background for my 2002 Journal Pages and tried to convey through color and texture the feeling that each month presents in the Pacific Northwest where I reside. This page represents July with its long summer days and saturated colors: gardens in full bloom, clear blue skies, and wonderful sunsets. I used beads for further emphasis and embellishment. Silk fusion is made by layering lengths of hand-dyed silk in overlapping rows until the desired thickness is achieved. It is then painted with a liquid textile medium which, when dry, holds it all together."

Marjorie A. DeQuincy

SACRAMENTO, CALIFORNIA

July 2004 (Top right)

"Low Tide Treasure"

"One of my favorite adventures is roving on the beach at low tide. So much glistening treasure is washed ashore. My QuiltPage interprets the tangled beauty of kelp, shells, polished pebbles, tumbled glass, and driftwood. The delight of 'the find' makes the whole world pink and rosy! I used Golden® paint; Sulky Holoshimmer®; and YLI Wonder Invisible® monofilament."

Gwyned Trefethen

SHERBORN, MASSACHUSETTS

May 2004 (Bottom right)

"I had saved a piece of floral chiffon for years, thinking that it would be intriguing to lay it over colored fabrics. I stitched together a Mondrian background of blocks of intensely colored fabrics and layered the chiffon on top, satin-stitching it down in channels with variegated thread. Next, I carefully cut away sections of chiffon to reveal the solid colors beneath. The satin stitching I used in the body of the quilt inspired me to finish the edge with a satin-stitch border. I felt playful and emboldened."

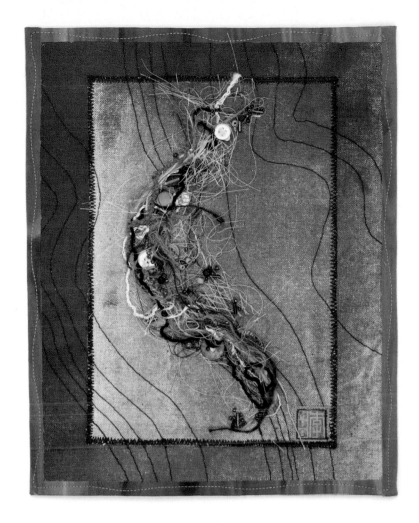

Lisa Konkel

RICHFIELD, MINNESOTA

(This page and opposite)

January 2006 (Top left)

"I carved a stamp and stamped the background, added a semi-transparent layer of painted WonderUnder® for the mid-ground, and then played with my soldering iron, sheer fabric, and fibers for the foreground images. The fabric medallions were made by sandwiching loose Angelina® fibers between two pieces of synthetic sheer fabric. I traced my design onto wash-away stabilizer, placed it on the fabric sandwich, and machine-stitched along the lines. I washed away the stabilizer and then used a soldering iron to burn away the fabric and fibers between the stitching lines."

August 2004 (Bottom left)

"I wanted to try something new with oil paint sticks and another abstract design. I used Shiva® Paintstiks® to color some funky white-on-white fabric, blending the colors so that there would be some flow in the final piece. I cut the fabric into squares and fused them onto black fabric in a grid pattern."

June 2005 (Opposite)

"I manipulated a photo of our screen door, with its wrought iron grid, in Photoshop® to get a line drawing, which I resized and printed onto a sheet of tear-away stabilizer. I made five layers: the stabilizer, painted Tyvek®, background fabric, batting, and backing fabric, and then machine-quilted along the lines. After removing the stabilizer, I used a heat gun to melt away and distress the excess Tyvek®."

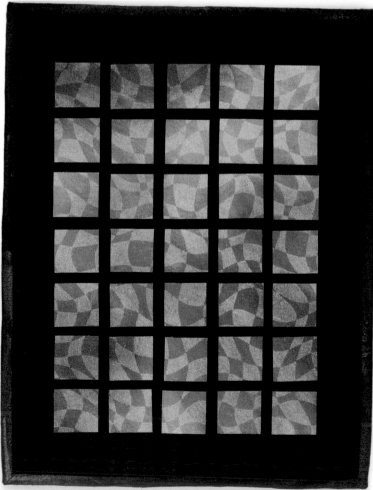

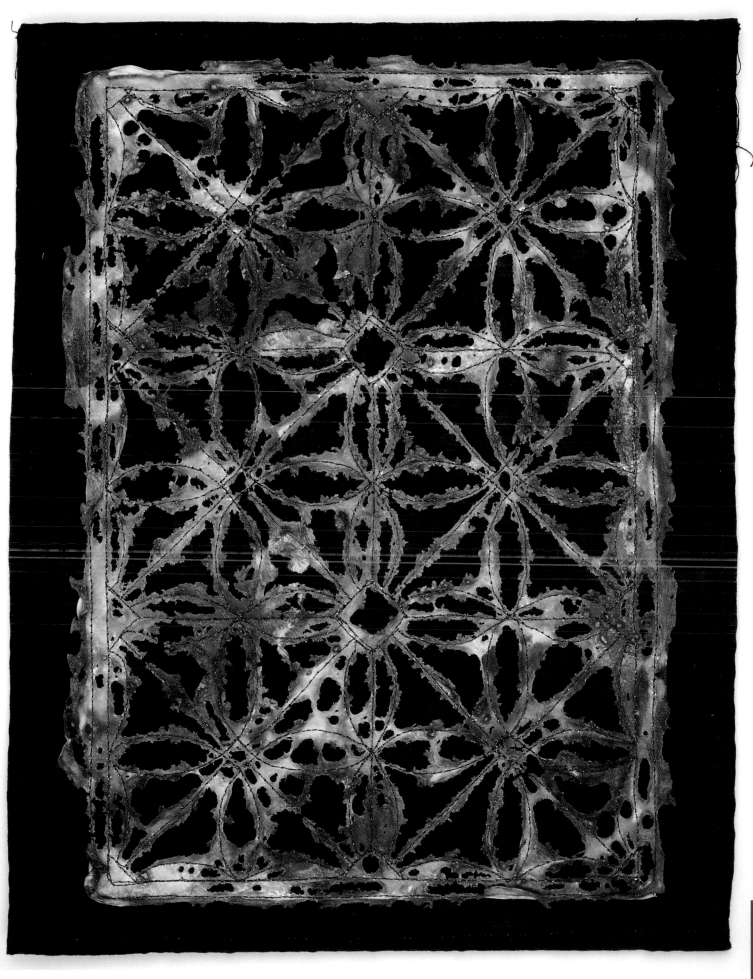

Creative Quilting: THE JOURNAL QUILT PROJECT

Linda Teddlie Minton

HOUSTON, TEXAS

February 2006 (Opposite)

"The Other Side of the Fence"

"I've been thinking recently about different ways of looking at the world, and this piece is about physical and emotional exclusion. Some of my friends are physically handicapped, and they necessarily see the world through different eyes. Although they have all experienced some type of exclusion at some point in their lives, they have each overcome various forms of negative preconceptions in order to strive toward their own highest potential. Some have already succeeded, and some are still striving...but all are heroes in my eyes."

April 2005 (Top right)

"Dragons Need Love, Too"

"After taking a class with Meena Schaldenbrand in Chicago, I came home and played with metals. It was surprising to learn that I could machine-sew through some metals! I loved the colorful results of heat on copper and the wonderful juxtaposition of hard metal against soft fabric. A slow sewing speed but no special sewing machine needle was needed to sew through these metals. The dragonflies were cut from a soda can and the copper mesh was made with a paper punch. Since the chain mail was very difficult to cut, I had to use heavy-duty tin snips."

Alyson M. Olander

ROCKVILLE, MARYLAND

January 2006 (Right)

"I moved my sewing space from one room to another in January 2006. As the room came back together I came up with the phrase 'from chaos comes order.' I applied fusible web to the backs of my fabrics, cut them into tiny pieces, and fused them to a foundation in a spiral pattern. The goal was to make a quilt that acted like a Van Gogh painting—tiny individual pieces that form into a beautiful whole as you step further away from it. I quilted the piece starting at the center, following the spiral pattern outwards, and added some beading to further define the spiral."

Gloria Hansen
HIGHTSTOWN, NEW JERSEY

January 2006

"January's journal started with two pieces of fabric that I dyed many years ago but recently monoprinted with fabric paints. It was fun breathing new life into the dyed fabric, and my goal was to create something abstract and free-form as a new start to the year. I cut curves freeform and arranged them onto the background. I also cut a wide strip from which I cut out geometric shapes. The piece seemed to need a bit of red; in my stash, I found some red scraps that I dyed some time ago."

Debbie Markowitz
JERUSALEM, ISRAEL

January 2006

"This is just one of those things that came into my head to try out—absolutely no symbolism here! In my stash, I found many one- to two-yard lengths of different yarns and hand-dyed fabric with a somewhat circular pattern. I had dyed the fabric with a pipe that was about 9" long and ¾" in diameter. I took a yellow fat quarter, held the pipe under the middle of the fabric, and pushed some of the fabric into the pipe opening. Then I gathered the fabric around the pipe tightly and wound string down the length of the pipe, pushing up a little so as to get most of the fabric covered. Then I put it in a dye solution of red and later took off the string and rinsed. Next, I wadded it up into a ball and weighted it down in a blue dye solution."

Virginia A. Spiegel
BYRON, ILLINOIS

May 2003 (Top right)

"Growing"

"In this QuiltPage, I sought significance and texture in simplicity. This painted, wholecloth design repeats the red spiral chosen as a unifying device and symbolizes energy that is felt throughout the year. May is when my landscape garden finally decides to shrug off the unsettled weather of April and really start to show its shape and color. Monoprinting was done using a light-weight piece of plastic that was painted with several colors of textile paint, marked using a variety of found objects, then placed paint-side down on previously painted fabric and rolled with light pressure."

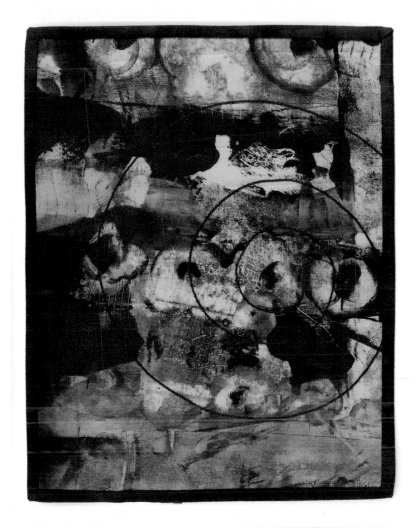

August 2003 (Bottom right)

"Portage"

"My previous Journal Quilts were layers and layers of fabric, so this year all of my Journal Quilts are painted, wholecloth compositions with the thoughts or events that inspired each month referenced in the title. The red spiral was repeated as the unifying device. August is the month my sister and I go voyaging in the Boundary Waters Canoe Area Wilderness. We paddle, portage, and once again, fall under the spell of the trees, water, and silence."

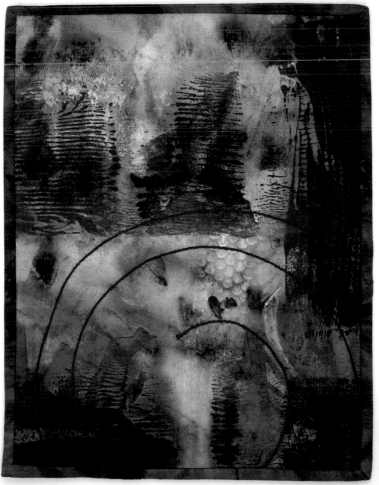

Creative Quilting: THE JOURNAL QUILT PROJECT

Linda J. Huff

ALGONQUIN, ILLINOIS

January 2003 (Opposite)

"At the mailbox today I noticed the water in the gutter was frozen over with ice. The rocks in the gutter punctured what would have been a smooth surface. There is ice everywhere, so ice became my theme for this QuiltPage. Using a black-and-gray mottled fabric, I fashioned rock shapes, stuffed them, and appliquéd them to the same mottled background. I started stitching using a straight stitch to outline the rocks and radiate out. Two spools of white thread and many hours later, I decided this was taking a really long time and began to try the specialty stitches on my machine that reminded me of ice to fill in more space, carefully following the same radiating stitches. After completing the stitching, I decided to press the piece so it would lay flat. Just as I started, my iron spewed out a big puddle of water in the lower right-hand corner...which began to take on a faint blue tinge. The backing fabric was bleeding and the thread was wicking the dye to the top of the piece! I stood there in despair and finally realized the effect was actually pretty! So I wet the entire quilt sandwich and allowed the loose dye from the backing fabric to stain the white thread. Since the threads are of differing blends they accepted the dye in varying degrees. Because of the gradation of colors in the dyes of the backing fabric, some thread looks gray or blue or purple, while the thread with the least amount of cotton remained white."

Pamela Burke

MIDDLETOWN, NEW JERSEY

September 2004 (Top right)

"I made this piece on September 11, 2004. Thirty-seven people from my town died in the World Trade Center attack. I used my own hand-painted fabrics including ripped cheesecloth. The sun print with feathers implies the scorched footprint of the towers that fell like feathers. I was thinking about how bloodless 9/11 seemed, and how the lifeblood evaporated in the extreme heat. I wondered how many more ashes of people around the world had been caught in the net of fear and retaliation released that day. I felt blessed to be able to spend this day expressing my feelings and remembering the beauty and goodness of life."

Eileen Doughty

VIENNA, VIRGINIA

August 2002 (Bottom right)

"The Grove of the Patriarchs, on the slope of Mount Rainier, is named for its thousand-year-old cedars, firs, and hemlocks. This is my homage to a fallen cedar. Its bark was gone, exposing the weathered wood. I mixed fabric paints to get the colors of weathered wood, pressed in small folds for a rougher texture, then machine-quilted to keep the folds down and indicate the grain of the wood. Even fallen, this tree invoked awe and inspired contemplation of the cycle of life, death, and rebirth."

Ivana Oblonsky Thomas
SALT LAKE CITY, UTAH

February 2004 (Left)

"I was hungry for color and sunshine. My challenge was to make a piece with all my fabrics in it—between 200 and 300, collected since my first quilt in 1975. They are all there, some stitched out of view, but there. It turned out to be a bit of a rainbow quilt; the bright colors were fun to work with as a contrast to the gray dreariness of the month."

Cynthia Wenslow
SANTE FE, NEW MEXICO

January 2006 (Bottom left)

"I have long been very interested in the study of complex adaptive systems and chaos theory. However, January 2006 was a month of turmoil on every front in my life... personal, professional, and physical. It brought it all a bit too close to home! This QuiltPage depicts my erratic cardiac status over a background of fused Koch curves, representing my effort to remember that even though the surface of things may look and feel chaotic, there is always an underlying order to all things, if we can only see."

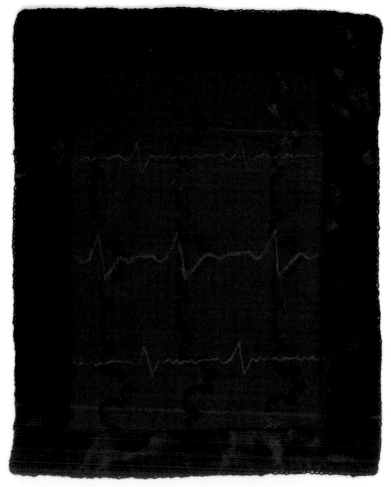

Karen E. Cote
WEBSTER, NEW YORK

January 2005 (Opposite)

"Sleet"

"Cold and freezing, with some sleeting snow—this month reminds me of the sleeting snow, getting heavier in Fibonacci sequence, which I've decided to study. A cold blue holds no yellow tone for warmth. To achieve the steam-textured silk I used in this piece, I wet and hand-twisted Shantung and Habotai silks into ropes so tightly that the silk twisted back upon itself. Once twisted, the ropes were microwaved in short bursts to dry them out—this resulted in both a steaming and drying action and set the texture. When dry, the ropes were untwisted and fused to a light backing to hold them in the desired position, and then cut into strips for insertion into the quilt."

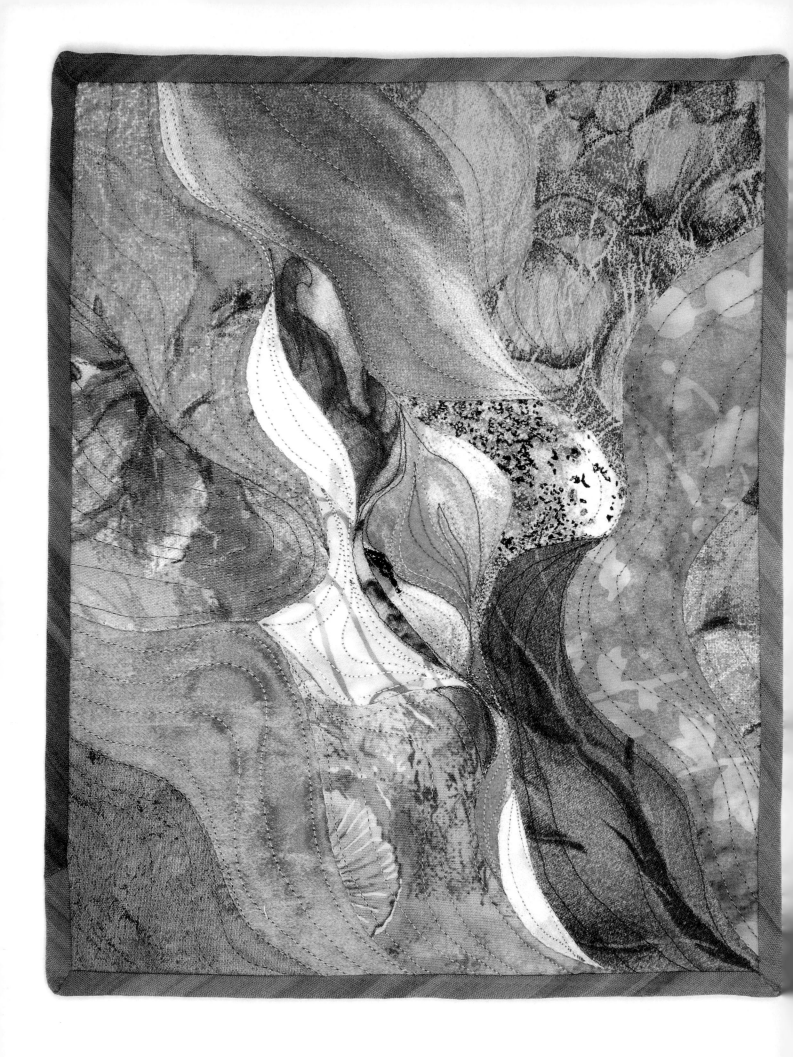

Creative Quilting: THE JOURNAL QUILT PROJECT

Judy B. Dales
GREENSBORO, VERMONT

January 2002 (Opposite)

"This design achieves the perfect balance between abstraction and representation, suggestive of a flower, but vague enough to be any or all flowers. I am enchanted with the ability of printed fabric to adapt, and I enjoy the transformation that happens when prints are viewed so intimately. They seem to blossom and take on a totally different character. The quilting line also achieves greater prominence in a diminutive piece and becomes proportionately more effective and important."

Daphne Greig
NORTH SAANICH,
BRITISH COLUMBIA, CANADA

September 2005 (Top right)

"I wanted to play with paint and stamps, so I gathered them, plus small squares of linen, silk, organza, pima cotton, and Ultrasuede®. The stamped squares were attached to the base fabric with wooden and clay beads. I bordered the QuiltPage with hand-painted fabric and added more stamping. It was interesting to see the results on different fabrics and textures. More play is planned!

Liz Jarr
ROSEMOUNT, MINNESOTA

February 2004 (Right)

"The Journal Quilt Project allowed me to explore a variety of techniques in a small format while going beyond unfinished samples. Here, fabric was dyed and marbled using shaving cream combined with fabric dyes. The circles were sewn with the fabric on the point of a thumbtack taped to the bed of the sewing machine. This caused the fabric to turn in a circle around the point. The circles were made with various stitches, couched threads, and bobbin drawing."

Roberta Chalfy Miller
SARASOTA, FLORIDA

January 2006

"I first did this journal quilt using only a few precious frayed threads of a three-inch square of the orange fabric from the Christo installation in New York's Central Park. This I scattered on my hand-painted blue background, but I realized that the contrast was insufficient. I am drawn to dupioni silk's fraying and shimmer, so I added rectangular blocks of orange/fuchsia dupioni, making a much stronger statement. I fell in love with the photos of the Christo installation, especially the bold orange against the bare trees and sky. I was successful in getting one of the few squares of Christo's fabric that the volunteer attendants gave out once a day. I had the square pinned to my design board for a long time before I could allow myself to use even part of it in anything."

Carol Cassidy
CHARLOTTESVILLE, VIRGINIA

January 2006

"'Indecision' is the theme of this piece for an art-quilt study group and also this month's QuiltPage. I wanted to try to weave fabric without having to piece. The background is hand-painted with mostly Setacolor fabric paints, but the background fabric is what I refer to as my 'drop cloth' for cleaning up leftover paint after a painting session. Different paints used over several years created this look, which was finally heat-set."

Meena Schaldenbrand

PLYMOUTH, MICHIGAN

February 2006

"Dreaming of Summer"

"Using gloves, safety glasses, and tin snips I cut apart aluminum drink cans around the text; I discarded the thick tops. Since I could not pin the metal, I taped one side of the metal edge to hold it in place and sewed on the opposite side. I started sewing slowly in the fabric part of the quilt right next to the metal before sewing on the cans. The cans are surprisingly thin and easy to sew. I used old size-12 needles."

July 2003

"Fourth of July Fireworks"

"Using aluminum soft drink cans sewn on the sewing machine was my experiment for this QuiltPage. To create my palette, I used scissors to cut up a CD with an NBC peacock logo; this provided me with the colors I needed. I used fiberglass window screen sewn over the palette to hold the CD parts in place."

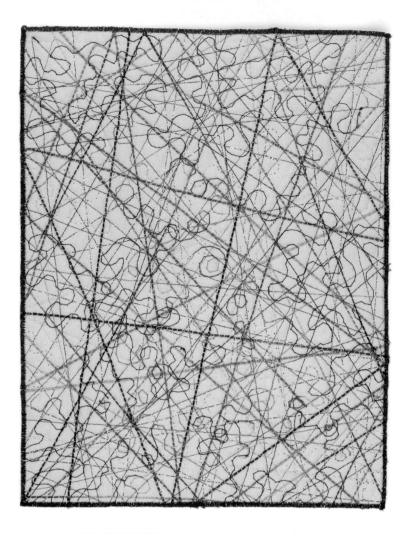

Cathy Neri
MILFORD, PENNSYLVANIA
January 2003 (Left)

"For this year's Journal Quilts, I decided to pay tribute to various (mostly modern) artists by re-interpreting their works in fabric and thread. For January, I chose Mark Tobey and his 'Advance of History'. This piece provided the opportunity to empty some leftover bobbins of their threads and yarns. Believe it or not, there are more than 50 different threads in and on this piece!"

Susan Pel-Or
NETANYA, ISRAEL
February 2006 (Bottom left)

"My journal quilts this year will recall the life of my husband who packed 90 years of living into only 71 years of life. They are all, very loosely, based on the Nine Patch. This February QuiltPage represents his teenage years, which were years of bicycles (he and his four cronies remained close friends with the friendships now being carried on by continuing generations) and B'nai Akiva (a youth group). To create this design, I used the sewing machine circle attachment with gold thread in the top, tight enough to bring up the black bobbin thread to form a stitch that gives the impression of a tire track."

Lily M. Kerns
MARIONVILLE, MISSOURI
January 2006 (Opposite)

"Fractals are a largely untapped design resource for quilters, and this quilt is printed from a fractal image that has been computer-manipulated to create fabric-like designs, otherwise unavailable to quilters. The pattern, created from a fractal made in Apophysis, was tiled in the program Kaleider, which also created the 'room' with the pattern on the walls in appropriate perspective. Extra batting was added under the ball area which is another Kaleider fabric using a different fragment from the same original fractal image. Minimal quilting helps keep the illusion of receding walls."

Debra Daw Lamm

CHENEY, WASHINGTON • *February 2006*

"Following Ruth Issett's fabric printing class I was inspired to make my own cloth. My original plan was to create one piece of cloth by mixing colors and creating pattern and then to quilt it creatively. I decided to take a riskier approach by making two pieces, cutting them freehand, and reconstructing them to make the final piece. To layer color and pattern on fabric, I made two different print blocks from puzzle pieces on a foam core base. On one piece of white fabric, I ironed on freezer-paper, puzzle-piece masks in a variety of sizes. I mixed more than 20 colors and varieties of Jacquard® paints. The first two layers of color were monoprinted and roller-printed. The masks were removed and I continued to add color in layers with the print block and hand painting."

Linda Salitrynski

ROME, PENNSYLVANIA • *February 2004*

"Several of the journal quilts from last year were wholecloth quilts done from my hand-dyed fabrics. I enjoyed doing them so much that I decided to create a set of four this year. This and the next three months all connect together, with the intention of having your eyes travel horizontally across all four. For this piece, I divided the quilt into different areas based upon color and machine-quilted them with matching rayon threads."

7: Abstract

Creative Quilting: THE JOURNAL QUILT PROJECT

Lynnae Ruske
FLAGSTAFF, ARIZONA

April 2005 (Opposite)

"A lecture on the seven layers of stitch inspired me to enhance the fabric. The first three layers consisted of the backing, batting, and wholecloth top. Number four was stitching around the motifs; number five was stamping and embossing additional spirals. Number six was more stitching, and number seven involved the placement of sheers on top and stitching around them."

Marilyn Rose
RIDGELAND, MISSISSIPPI

September 2005 (Top right)

"Fireworks"

"My small-scale version of the class project for Helen Marshall's class by the same name at Quilt University online provided my first experiment with free-motion machine embroidery on a pieced and stabilized background of various commercial star prints. So, now I can relive the joy and wonder of a delightful fireworks display every time I look at it! Here I have applied techniques I learned: free-motion machine embroidery on a pieced background, the importance of using stabilizers, and how to blend colors of rayon threads in layers to add depth to the actual explosions."

Cynthia Ann Morgan
BOULDER, COLORADO

February 2006 (Right)

"I'm experimenting with abstract ideas this year, using different colors and compositions to stretch myself. Using strips from another 'deconstructed' painted piece, I wove them into a colorful maze and added some dots for contrast in color and shape. What did I learn? Use everything, have no expectations, and be ready to be surprised!"

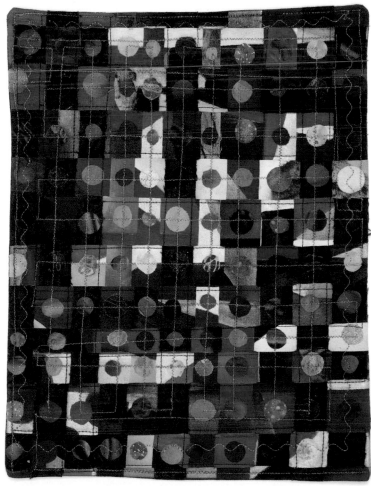

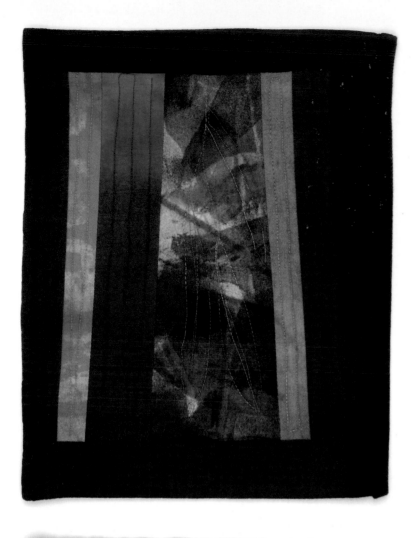

Giny Dixon
DANVILLE, CALIFORNIA

January 2006 (Left)

"I had learned to paint with dyes by apprenticing to L. Carlene Raper. Finally I was brave enough to cut into my own dye-painted fabrics to create a large wall hanging. A resist of eucalyptus leaves with thickened Procion® dyes created the focus fabric. I tried various thread and stitch combinations before quilting the large piece."

Claire Anne Gabrielsen Teagan
HIGHLAND, MICHIGAN

January 2003 (Bottom left)

"This year started off with new creative energy, particularly in my enthusiasm for the use of sheer fabrics. I painted a pair of old sheer drapes with Setacolor and sea salt and used that for the sheer circles, cutting away the back and batting. I made each third fully quilted and attached them using free-motion zigzag stitches. The curtains came out so beautifully that I wish I could hang them up again!"

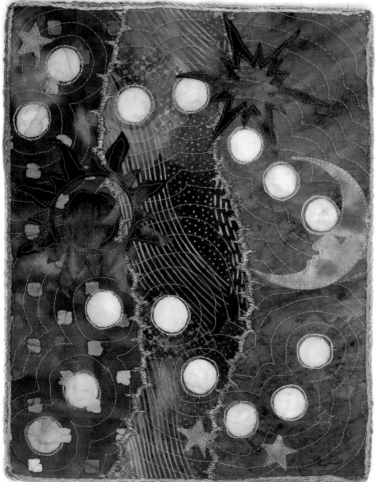

Magda Ann Clark
NORTH POLE, ALASKA

July 2005 (Opposite)

"Calypso"

"I really had fun with this piece. After stamping copper paint onto the fabric, I wove small fabric-like pieces with metallic cord using two different size Weavettes® and created 'people' with wire wrapped in colorful fibers. Everything was glued to the quilt top and embellished with feathers and rhinestone rings for glitz. My hubby, Brad, was delighted with this QuiltPage and named it 'Calypso' for its happy, festive colors and dancing figures."

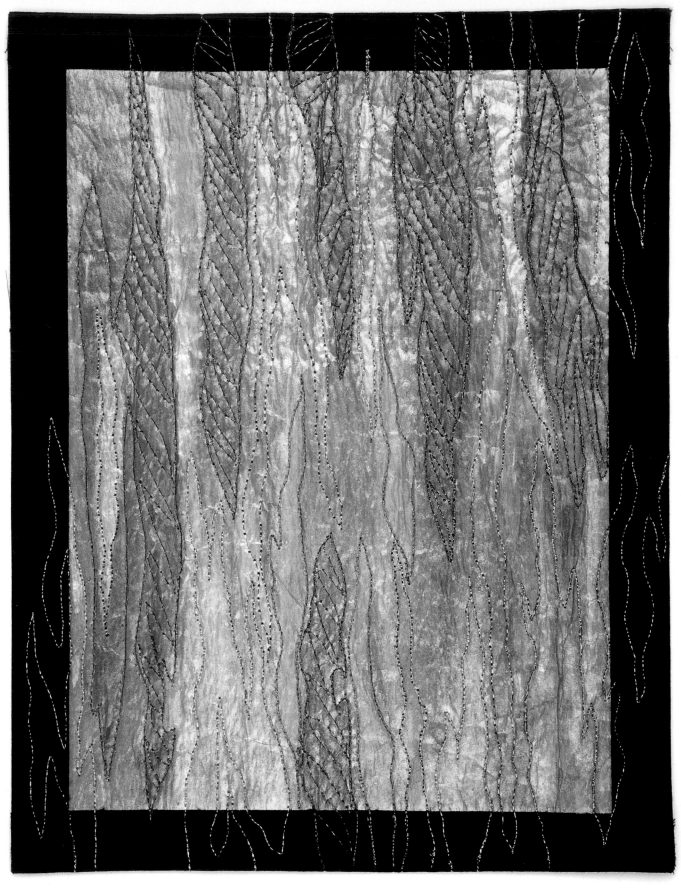

Marilyn Gillis

SHELBURNE, VERMONT • *April 2003*

"This month, continuing my experiments using paper in my quilts, I painted damp tissue paper with Pearl Ex® powders and brushed them out until they blended on the edges. After the paper dried, I fused it to batting and backing and then quilted it with metallic threads. I love the iridescent quality produced by the powders."

Marilyn Gillis

SHELBURNE, VERMONT • *June 2003*

"For this quilt I used layers of tissue paper. First I wet the paper, then added paints to create a watercolor effect, and drew pen markings. I added doily paper that was painted copper, cut into triangles, then quilted with copper metallic thread. To create a raised center I dampened tissue paper, added paint, crumpled the paper, and then stitched it on."

7: Abstract

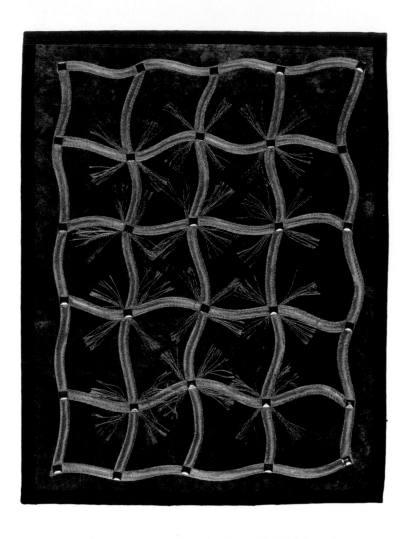

Diane Becka

NORTH BEND, WASHINGTON

January 2006 (Left)

"This year I want to focus on line and pattern—different ways of creating lines and different patterns resulting from those lines. I also want to try different embellishment techniques. This month I used wavy lines of gold bias on a black background painted with gold Lumiere® to create a freeform interwoven grid, accented with gold thread fringes and square, metal nail heads."

February 2006 (Bottom left)

"Here I worked with assorted colors and sizes of cut silk squares, arranging and interweaving them over a batik background over-painted with pearl white Lumiere® paint. Embellishment includes metallic thread for the quilting and silver metallic nail heads to accent the quilting lines."

Bonnie B. Ouellette

SENECA, SOUTH CAROLINA

January 2006 (Opposite)

"The explosive colors of Maui orchids inspired this piece. When you visit Hawaii, it is so tempting to see the wonderful plants but you cannot bring them home with you due to agricultural restrictions. I decided to bring them home in my journal quilt. I used abstract shapes inspired by my admiration of the work of Kandinsky to convey my mental images of Maui orchids. This piece contains hand-dyed fabric, hand-beaded embellishment, and chicken-scratch quilting, a technique learned from Susan Shie."

Creative Quilting: THE JOURNAL QUILT PROJECT

Steph Winn

LAS VEGAS, NEVADA

February 2003 (Opposite)

"I felt the love of my children and their quiet, warm hearts. I feel so lucky to have my family. Each one is different, each one special; all are happy and content. For this piece, I used fancy fibers, micro glass balls, the chenille technique, couching, and raw-edge appliqué."

Mary Beth Frezon

BRAINARD, NEW YORK

September 2003 (Top right)

"This completed my year of stretching my machine-quilting techniques each month. My starting theme was 'It's about the quilting!' I highly recommend small pieces as a way to experiment in technique. I played with thread color, different battings, stippling, and design, and really benefited from doing these each month. My September QuiltPage was an experiment in reverse appliqué and in the effect of really close stitching."

Francyne Willby

ATHENS, GEORGIA

January 2006 (Bottom right)

"Fabrications I"

"Although most of my work is representational, in 2006 I chose to concentrate on abstract and non-representational pieces to stretch my artistic expression. This wholecloth quilt is composed of my hand-dyed fabric and features stamping with paint. Commercial stamps and found objects were used to create an illusion of depth. The quilting is done with metallic thread in vertical lines spaced $1/8$" apart to increase the depth of field."

Kathy Angel Lee
OLD ORCHARD BEACH, MAINE

January 2006 (Top left)

"This quilt was started during a raging snowstorm when I'd really had enough snow already! The figure in the lower right is me trying to keep up with shoveling the swirling snow. To become part of the snowstorm, lots of small pieces of white and off-white fabric were snipped onto a blue-gray background. The person was purposely made small to emphasize the overwhelming feeling of the storm. To continue the snow theme, I cut the top a bit smaller than the backing and batting and distressed the edges of the batting to look like snow."

Linda Curtis Zimmerman
MADISON, CONNECTICUT

January 2006 (Bottom left)

"Coming Out From Behind"

"At the beginning of this year, I decided that every day I would spend time doing what I love —creating with textiles. My first exercise was to sew strips of scrap fabric in simple straight lines. After a few strips, it looked as though the woman in the center was peeking out from behind curtains or louvers. I kept going. This piece has become a symbol to me, a reminder to take risks and not remain hidden."

Claudia Castellanos Comay
SAN RAMON, CALIFORNIA

January 2006 (Opposite)

"Boxes, Boxes everywhere
A life contained
waiting, waiting
Rock, Paper, Scissors" —ccphus

"After a sudden, difficult move, I found myself with my entire household and my studio packed in boxes. Six months later, my daily life had reached a balance with a sufficient amount unpacked, but my art life, indeed my soul, lay mostly still sealed within those brown boxes. I moved them around like a baby playing with blocks, unable to find the space or even the emotional fortitude to deal with them. When 2006 began, I determined to begin anew, cutting the unnecessary and letting go. The Journal Quilt Project provided me a structure within which I could forge ahead. I have made a quilt page for every week so far, finding within them the strength to proceed fearlessly. For this QuiltPage, I chose a hand-painted background and a printing technique learned from Fran Skiles. I used a watercolor crayon to draw an image onto Pellon® Stitch-n-Tear and then printed it onto white fabric with a squeegee and gloss medium. I preserved the white by the use of the gloss medium and by adding gesso. Once the print was dry, I went back to it and judiciously applied color with diluted silk paint."

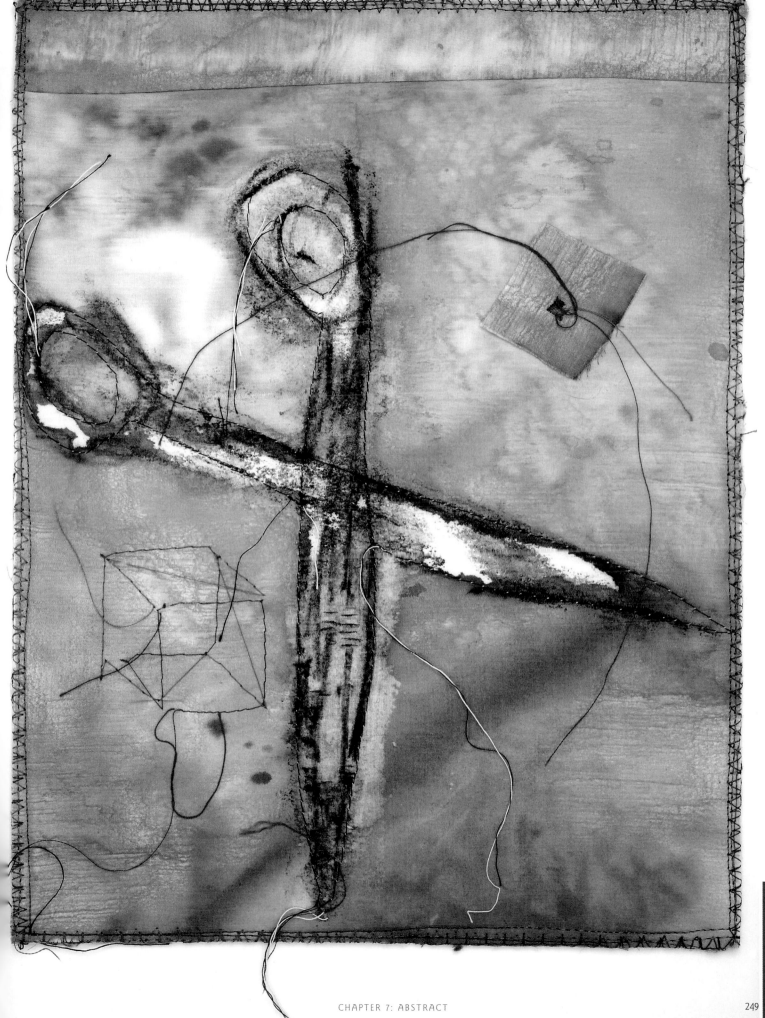

Creative Quilting: THE JOURNAL QUILT PROJECT

Frances Holliday Alford

AUSTIN, TEXAS

January 2005 (Opposite)

"My fascination with embellishment gave me the inspiration to work with only color in mind. Starting with a rainbow order series, I used only shades of red with every predominantly red object I could find—red beads, buttons, souvenirs, rubber pieces, jewelry, found objects— to make a solid gleaming rectangle. I used a Timtex™ base covered with batting and fabric."

Virginia O'Donnell

PORTLAND, OREGON

August 2004 (Top right)

"In two days in a Carol Soderlund workshop, 12 of us dyed 1,029 color samples using exact formulas. I couldn't bear not to use the last bits of my share of the samples, so I fused tiny pieces in gradations on hand-painted fabric. It turned out to provide me with a wonderful reminder of a fantastic learning experience."

Karen Stiehl Osborn

OMAHA NEBRASKA

September 2002 (Right)

"Running with the Wind"

"Am I running away from the year I've had, or running towards my new artistic freedom? This journal began with a tangle of threads from the dryer that were too gorgeous to throw away. As I played and pulled apart the threads, they began to take the shape of a woman running. It seemed very symbolic for the year I was having. I layered some sheers to add wind and motion and added some bright-colored snippets to symbolize hope for the future."

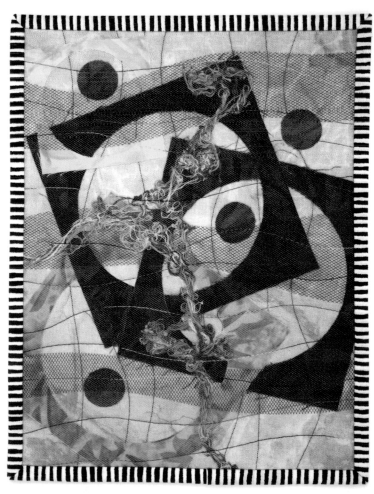

Stacy Hurt
ORANGE, CALIFORNIA

January 2005 (Left)

"I found myself drawn to further developing my calligraphic art and using it as surface design for my art quilting. The word 'Wonder' was chosen for how it looked as well as its meaning for the new year."

Linda K. Hayes
BATAVIA, ILLINOIS

April 2005 (Bottom left)

"Reading through past journal entries over the years, I found many references to leisurely walks shared with my husband. Having just enjoyed a beautiful afternoon with him, it felt appropriate to record it in fabric. Using a small zigzag stitch, I free-motion stitched a recent journal entry onto a piece of my hand-dyed fabric with variegated thread. Zigzagged edges serve as the binding, something new for me."

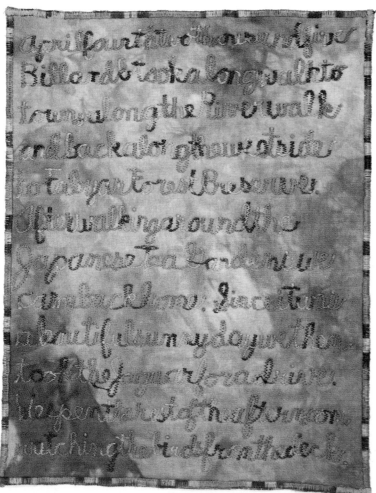

Jennifer Beaven
ACTON, MASSACHUSETTS

May 2005 (Opposite)

"A friend and I had decided to use Celtic runes as a theme for our journal quilts. 'Teiwaz' is a rune of responsibility and knowing one's own strengths. This quilt includes the responsible crow that cares for her comrades, the strength of my hand-carved stamps, and a seasonal need to push boundaries with unconventional materials. I started with a page of plastic pockets designed for coin storage. By typing, stamping, drawing, and rummaging, I created a set of related symbols and images on small squares of paper. I filled each plastic pocket with a paper square and then sewed them shut with a simple zigzag on my trusty old Singer®."

For centuries, the **practice** of counting crows, or crow augury, has been said to **predict** the future.

For centuries, the **practice** of counting crows, or crow augury, has been said to **predict** the future.

Cynthia Paugh St. Charles

BILLINGS, MONTANA • *March 2004*

"This QuiltPage was an experimental springboard for a large quilt that was in the works. I needed to work through the design process for an idea portraying mammograms with an underlying theme related to breast cancer survivors. I used a discharge process that resulted in breast-like, black-and-white images. To make the image on this journal quilt, black cotton was wrapped around a stone and held in place with a rubber band. The fabric was dipped into household bleach, and when the desired amount of color was removed, the fabric was rinsed in cold water, followed by soaking to stop the bleaching action."

Sherrie Tootle

GARLAND, TEXAS • *February 2006*

"In this QuiltPage, I was trying to capture the western exposure glowing through a stained glass piece made for me by my friend Linda. I added small pieces of shimmer organza to the hand-dyed fabric squares using Bo-Nash to add sheen and sparkle. Everything was then covered with tulle. Additional glow was added by scribbling with several colors of the wax crayons."

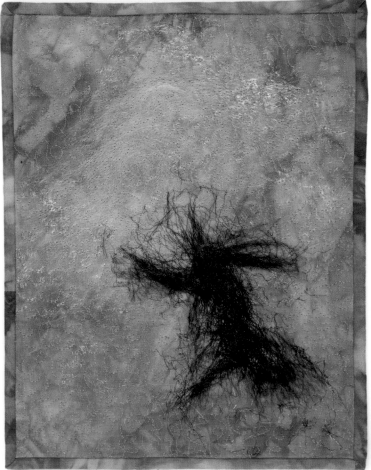

Irish Casey-Green
COLONIAL HEIGHTS, VIRGINIA

January 2006 (Left)

"How to take my longstanding obsession of photographing doors and windows and interpret it in fabric? I saw a window full of bottles in a junk shop and puzzled over how to convey the image. The solution? Batiks became light-filled bottles! And all the new stuff to use—Angelina®—I'm loving it! I saw the chatter about netting on QuiltArt—should I add a cobweb to balance the bottles? Organza is too crisp—maybe tear it? Are there mistakes? Or just happy accidents and opportunities to improvise?"

Beverly J. Hart
SPANISH FORK, UTAH

February 2005 (Bottom left)

"Running in Circles"

"I played at layering and creating shapes with Angelina® fibers without any kind of directions. When the runner appeared, I knew I had the start of my QuiltPage. That's me—always running, and frayed around the edges. Being home only on weekends, the stress of selling this house—it's all taken its toll. I love the iridescence of the fibers and the way they look on my hand-dyed fabric."

Lyric Montgomery Kinard
CARY, NORTH CAROLINA

January 2002 (Opposite)

"Contrast"

> *"Introspection, Effusiveness. Veriditas and
> Rock Stillness.
> Green Winter in a Blanket of White Snow."*

"In thinking of the snow flying in on a green Carolina landscape, I tried to capture that swirling whiteness using pearlescent Lumiere® textile paint both as a first layer and after the stitching was completed. Shimmering white organza was also cut into slivers and fused into swirls; darker organza added depth and shadows. Not quite satisfied yet, I used 007 Bonding Agent® (like WonderUnder® in a salt shaker) and fused specks of silver foil to the quilt to add more brightness."

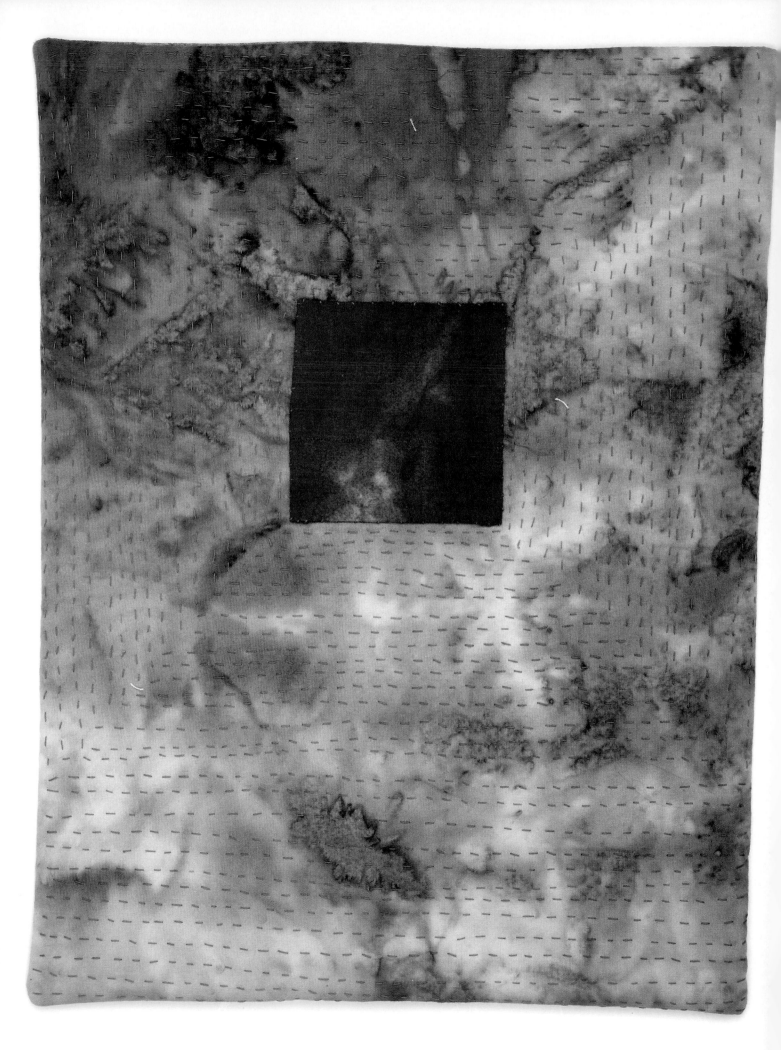

Creative Quilting: THE JOURNAL QUILT PROJECT

Sue Lemmo
CLEARFIELD, PENNSYLVANIA

February 2006 (Opposite)

"During the winter months, I get claustrophobic under the cold gray skies of Pennsylvania. Through these small pieces I am seeking to satisfy my spirit's need to float freely in the universe. They are a means of escape from the day-to-day obligations of a middle-aged working mother. The act of creating these pages is meditative for me."

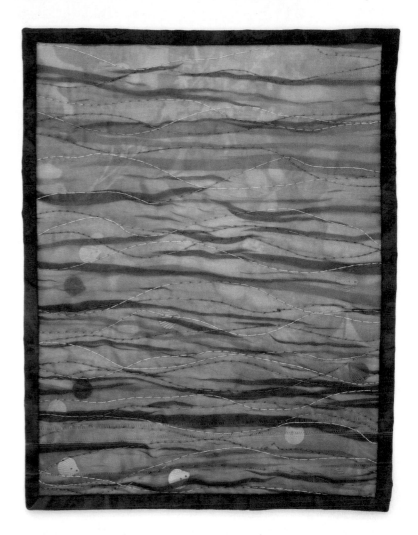

Heather G. Stoltz
WOODBRIDGE, CONNECTICUT

January 2006 (Top right)

"The focus of this month was my trip to Mexico. This quilt, therefore, reflects the tranquility of the ocean waves, warm breezes, and sunshine of my vacation on the beach. Two different shades of blue organza were placed on top of yellow cotton fabric, catching seashell sequins between the layers. All of the layers are held together with free motion quilting using variegated threads."

Sandra Wagner
PINE GROVE, CALIFORNIA

January 2006 (Right)

"This QuiltPage is based on a picture I took of the Power Fire that was burning out of control here where we live. Smoke filled the sky with an eerie orange glow, distorting shapes and colors of the sun, sky, and trees. Working with my print in Paint Shop Pro®, I manipulated the electronic image."

Judith Lundberg
SILVER SPRING, MARYLAND

July 2003 (Left)

"I decided to use a theme for 2003—'Arches and Openings'. July was an 'Openings' month. The colors suggest hot and sultry, not unusual weather in the Washington, D.C., area. I used scraps left over from a guild challenge using stripes, dots, and plaids as the background for this page. I cut it off-kilter for interest, then added threadpainting circles or openings as part of the quilting. I cut freezer-paper circles and ironed them on, meander-quilted around them, then added the thread-painted circles on top of that."

Kathy Harben
HAYESVILLE, NORTH CAROLINA

July 2004 (Bottom left)

"Western Wildfires"

"In July, every time I turned on the TV and saw the destruction taking place in the West, my heart went out to those brave souls living in fear of the huge fires. This is my tribute to them. The quilt was made with cotton corduroy fabric I hand-dyed using Procion® dyes. I always use the instructions from Ellen Anne Eddy's THREAD MAGIC when I dye fabric because it is so well written."

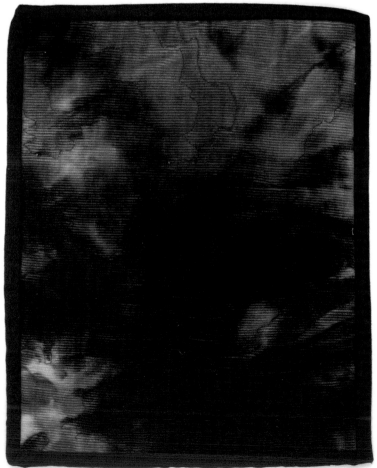

Peggy Daley Spence
TULSA, OKLAHOMA

April 2003 (Opposite)

"Most of my work this year I called 'rag picking,' using unwanted scraps to create something new. Using what was 'only trash' freed me up to experiment and risk new things. After all, if it turns out badly who cares? I took what I would normally consider insipid calico prints and ripped them into strips and arranged them from dark to light to represent the soil and growth bursting with life. A found stamped image seemed to complete the story of growth going on in my life at this time."

Larkin Jean Van Horn

WHIDBEY ISLAND, WASHINGTON

April 2004 (Opposite)

"My husband is a writer and incredibly fussy about proper word use, grammar, punctuation, and spelling. I found a book in his office called COMMAS ARE OUR FRIENDS, and I knew I had to use the lowly comma as the focus of a journal quilt. I threw in a liberal dose of dots for good measure, which would turn the comma into a semi-colon, stand alone as a period, or pair up as a colon. One-inch strips were woven for the background and secured with a fusible interfacing. Heavy metallic threads were couched over the intersections, and the appliqué shapes were added by machine."

February 2006 (Top right)

"I visited Italy, France, and Spain in 1999, and saw this shape of window in many cathedrals and monasteries. Some were elaborate and busy stained glass representations of times past; others were merely clear or colored glass. I chose some simple motifs for my window, forms that seem to show up in my work on a regular basis— fish, leaves, figures, and spirals. To achieve the depth of color, the hand-dyed silk organza is layered over the dyed cotton. I cut the organza larger than the cotton base and allowed it to crinkle and fold over itself while machine stitching, gaining even more depth."

Martha Sielman

STORRS, CONNECTICUT

April 2002 (Right)

"Slipping"

"The first Journal Quilt Project was incredibly inspirational. Working on fiber art is very time-intensive. It's difficult to try new ideas when each piece takes weeks or months to create. Working on the Journal Quilts allowed me to feel free to experiment, to play. This piece expresses how that freedom allowed me to slip outside of the too-rigid rules within which I had been working."

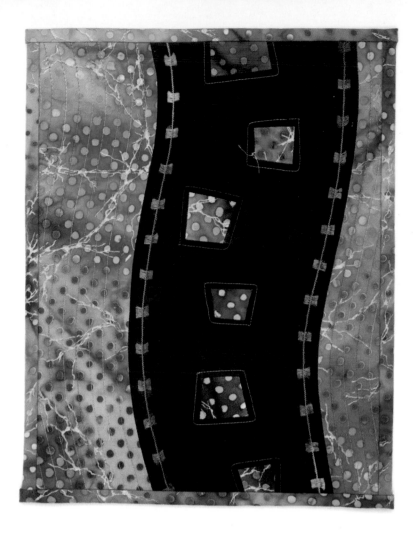

Suzanne Freed
ATLANTA, GEORGIA

February 2006 (Top left)

"I collect quilt books, tucking away ideas to use 'someday.' I decided that 2006 would be my 'someday' to play with some of the techniques and embellishments that I've collected over the years. In February, I did one of the exercises in Dianne S. Hire's QUILTERS PLAYTIME GAMES WITH FABRICS and then had more fun couching with a friend's leftover yarn. After completing a 'run' of fabrics in Dianne's Hopscotch game, I curve-pieced it and added decorative yarn by couching with monofilament thread."

Sherrie Spangler and Julia Spangler DesertSpring
ROCKFORD, ILLINOIS

September 2003 (Bottom left)

"Julia's Dreamtime"

"My daughter, Julia Spangler DesertSpring, was born in September; this quilt honors her free spirit. I copied one of her colored pencil drawings (done when she was 14) and my text onto heat-transfer paper and ironed it onto sheer yellow fabric, then layered that over cotton that Julia had painted the previous summer. I quilted swirls with invisible thread."

Sherrie Spangler
ROCKFORD, ILLINOIS

May 2003 (Opposite)

"My challenge this year was to explore layering. I tried to recreate the azaleas, lilacs, ferns, and washes of sunlight outside my window by layering shimmering, sheer fabrics and anchoring them with sweeping lines of gold quilting and stamping. I let the thread tails dangle to reflect more light and added a scattering of beads."

CHAPTER 7: ABSTRACT

7. Abstract

Stacey McElheny Conover
SEDALIA, MISSOURI

June 2005

"As part of my commitment to try new techniques in the Journal Quilts, I started with black cotton fabric, placed rocks on the fabric, drew the fabric around the rocks, and held it tightly in place with rubber bands. Then I squirted bleach on the rocks. The bleach did not penetrate where the rubber bands were, but did discharge the fabric covering the rocks, as well as around the base of the rocks. After neutralizing the fabric, I used a gold Procion® dye to over-dye it. I fussy-cut a starburst from it to create the QuiltPage."

Carrie Beauchamp
ALEXANDRIA, VIRGINIA

July 2003

"Memory"

"I heard an interview with Isabelle Allende where she said that memory, and therefore storytelling, is black and white—we remember the good times and bad, but not the mundane. I used that idea in this quilt, and congregated the darker stories towards the center. I also added bits of color for those discrete sensual memories that are not necessarily a part of a story—the grassy tang of rhubarb, the color of fingers dyed purple from blackberry picking, the metallic, rubbery smell of water from the garden hose on a hot day in July."

Mary Louise Smith

BROOKLYN, NEW YORK

March 2003

"A strip of batik fabric from Spain was my inspiration for creating this design. It echoed the memory of my trip there many years ago. I hand-painted additional complementary fabrics that conveyed my impression of the vibrancy of Spain's rich culture and people. Turquoise metallic threads with red and gray suede free-flowing ribbons add sparkle and movement as in Spain's pulsating rhythms."

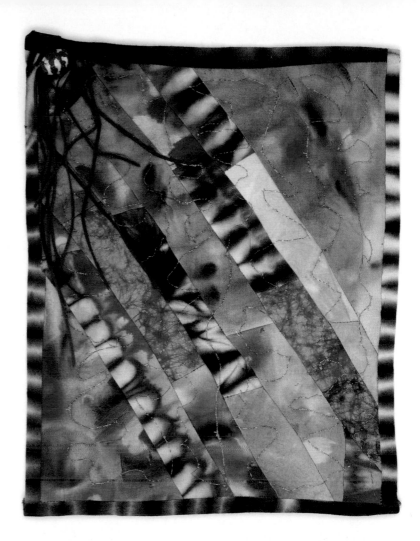

Michele M.A. David, MD

CHESTNUT HILL, MASSACHUSETTS

September 2003

"I decided not to have a theme for the 2003 journal quilts. Instead, I wanted to explore a variety of techniques and put my feelings on fabrics. I was inspired by the colors of a wonderful sunset in Newport, Rhode Island, to make this quilt. Working small scale allowed me to try many more techniques than usual. I might have otherwise felt too overwhelmed to start. Working from memory, I painted the QuiltPage using Lumiere® liquid acrylic paints on handmade paper to recall the colors of the sunset that struck me."

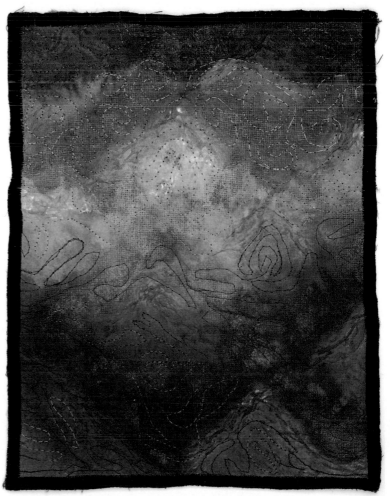

Jette Clover

ANTWERPEN, BELGIUM • *September 2002*

"I have totally fallen in love with yellow—from pale whitish yellow to deep bronze. My goal was to simplify by using only one color, and I wanted my last QuiltPage of the year to remind me that 'less is more.' The pages are all done. I am, however, far from being done with yellow. I am struggling to keep up with my own demand for yellow cloth, and I have to dye fabric several times a week. My monochromatic use of yellow might become permanent..."

Jette Clover

ANTWERPEN, BELGIUM • *April 2003*

"I use horizontal lines extensively in my work, to provide a feeling of stability and security, like a horizon. I decided to experiment with vertical lines and see if I could combine the two directions. Maybe this could be the start of exploring depth. I used transparent fabrics, screen-printing, and slashing."

7: Abstract

Artist Index

Bibliography

**THE ART OF ANNEMIEKE MEIN,
WILDLIFE ARTIST IN TEXTILES**
Annemieke Mein
Search Press, 2001
ISBN: 0855329777

THE BUTTERFLY
Paul Starosta (photographer) and
Jean-Pierre Vesco
Studio, 2001
ISBN: 0670030465

COMMAS ARE OUR FRIENDS
Joe Devine
Green Stone Publications, 1988
ISBN: 1882010078

**CREATIVE MARBLING ON FABRIC,
A GUIDE TO MAKING ONE OF A KIND FABRICS**
Judy Simmons
Martingale & Co., Inc., 1999
ISBN: 156477256X

INVISIBLE APPLIQUÉ
Ami Simms
Mallery Press, 2nd edition 1988
ISBN: 0943079012

JAMES HERRIOT'S YORKSHIRE
James Herriot
St. Martin's Press, Inc, 1979
ISBN: 0312439717

LOS ANGELES: BIOGRAPHY OF A CITY
Caughey, J. and Berkeley, L., Ed.
University of California Press, 1977
ISBN: 0520034104

MAKE YOUR OWN CONTEMPORARY QUILTS
Paola Pieroni (photographer)
Hachette Illustrated, 2006
ISBN: 1844301125

**MICKEY LAWLER'S SKYDYES:
A VISUAL GUIDE TO FABRIC PAINTING**
Mickey Lawler
C & T Publishing, 1999
ISBN: 157120072X

PAPER, METAL & STITCH
By Maggie Grey and Jane Wild
Chrysalis Books, 2004
ISBN: 0713489189

PICTURE THIS: HOW PICTURES WORK
Molly Garrett Bang
Chronicle Books, 2000
ISBN: 1587170299

**PIECED CURVES, SO SIMPLE: THE 6-MINUTE
CIRCLE AND OTHER TIME SAVING DELIGHTS**
Dale Fleming
C&T Publishing, 2005
ISBN: 1571202935

QUILTERS PLAYTIME GAMES WITH FABRICS
Dianne S. Hire
American Quilters Society, 2004
ISBN: 1574328263

QUILTED MEMORIES
Lesley Riley
Sterling/Chapelle, 2005
ISBN: 140271484X

QUILTING ARTS MAGAZINE®, ISSUE 17
Artist Profile: Marcy Tilton, page 40
Quilting Arts, LLC, 2005
ISSN: 1538-4950

QUILTING ARTS MAGAZINE®, ISSUE 19
Quilting Arts, LLC, 2005
ISSN: 1538-4950

**RAISED EMBROIDERY, A PRACTICAL GUIDE TO
DECORATIVE STUMPWORK**
Roy Hirst and Barbara Hirst
Rutland Group, 1995
ISBN: 1853912034

**READY-TO-USE PORTRAITS OF FAMOUS PEOPLE :
121 DIFFERENT COPYRIGHT-FREE ILLUSTRATIONS
PRINTED ONE SIDE**
Charles Hogarth
Dover Publications, 1994
ISBN: 0486282295

SURFACES FOR STITCH
Gwen Hedley
Quilters' Resource, Inc., Reprint edition 2000
ISBN: 1889682187

THREAD MAGIC
Ellen Anne Eddy
Quilting Arts LLC, Reprint edition 2005
ISBN: 0976692813

About the Editor

Karey Patterson Bresenhan is the president of Quilts, Inc. and director of the International Quilt Markets and International Quilt Festivals. Karey's business acumen, enthusiasm for quilting, and perseverance helped her create and foster the quilting industry, now worth $2.27 billion a year in the U.S. and involving 21.3 milliom American quilters.

An acknowledged expert on quilt dating, Karey was named to the Quilters' Hall of Fame and is the author or co-author of five quilt reference books and guest curator of museum exhibitions.

Karey and her cousin Nancy O'Bryant Puentes, along with their mothers, co-founded the prestigious International Quilt Association. Karey and Nancy continued their partnership to form The Alliance for American Quilts as well as co-direct Patchwork and Quilt Expo in Europe—the major international quilt show held in Europe since 1988.